GHOULARDI

Inside Cleveland TV's Wildest Ride

BY TOM **FERAN** AND R. D. **HELDENFELS**

GRAY & COMPANY, PUBLISHERS
CLEVELAND

Gray & Company, Publishers
1588 E. 40th St.
Cleveland, OH 44103
(216) 431-2665
www.grayco.com

Library of Congress cataloging-in-publication data
Feran, Tom.
Ghoulardi: Inside Cleveland TV's Wildest Ride /
Tom Feran and R. D. Heldenfels. —1st ed.
Includes bibliographical references and index.
1. Anderson, Ernie. 2. Television personalities—United States—Biography.
 3. Television broadcasting—Ohio—Cleveland—History.
 4. Shock theater. I. Heldenfels, R. D. II Title
PN1992.4.A48F47 1997
791.45'028'092—dc21   [B]   97-33803

ISBN 1-886228-18-3

Printed in the United States of America
10 9 8 7 6 5 4 3 2 1
First Edition

FOR ERNIE

"It takes a lot of talent... to get just the right muck."

The Chapter Is Ova Dey!

Acknowledgments

Our many thank-yous begin with Chuck Schodowski, Ernie Anderson's successor, friend, and curator, who immediately agreed to cooperate in our writing of this book and who spent hours in interviews, follow-up conversations, and other assistance, notably access to his collection of videotapes, photographs, and memorabilia.

Without his assistance, this book might never have happened. Without access to his archives, we might never have resolved some of the myths of the Ghoulardi era, such as the notion that only eighteen minutes of Ghoulardi footage survived. As we learned, the eighteen minutes referred only to Ernie as Ghoulardi speaking to the audience. In fact, hours of material exist, including filmed skits, four installments of "Parma Place," and Ernie's "interview" with Ghoulardi; seeing all that helped make this a better book. (A list of material viewed is in the bibliography.)

Three other people who saw Ghoulardi in his prime were also very helpful: Ron Sweed, who also shared his time, memories, and memorabilia; Bob Soinski, whose contribution to the making of Ghoulardi has often been overlooked; and Ralph Tarsitano, who was especially helpful in detailing the adventures of the Ghoulardi All-Stars. Ralph Gulko, another forgotten figure in the Ghoulardi story, brought to light new information about Ghoulardi's origins.

Thanks as well to WJW (Channel 8), notably Mike Renda and Kevin Salyer, which granted permission for this book but, like everyone else contacted, set no preconditions about content.

Other people who assisted in the making of this book include Paul Anderson, Katie Byard, Drew Carey, Jim Carney, Don (Kaptin Ignatz) Clark, Tim Conway, Mark Dawidziak, Mike Douglas, Bob Ferguson, Woody Fraser, Cristina Ferrare, David Giffels, Dick Goddard, Ray Harrison, Harvey Holocker, Howard Hoffmann, Dave Little, Rose Marie, Chris Quinn, Jack Riley, Sheldon Saltman, Linn Sheldon, Mary Strassmeyer, Rita Vennari, and Michael J. Weldon.

Bob Dyer of the *Akron Beacon Journal* not only conducted an extensive interview with Ernie Anderson, he generously shared the tape of the complete interview. Mike Olszewski of WOIO (Channel 19) and WUAB (Channel 43) made available the complete videotape of his 1996 interview, believed to be Ernie's last.

The Cleveland Press Collection at the Cleveland State University Archives was a valuable resource. Our thanks to CSU archivist Bill Becker for his aid in the project. Additionally, the microfilm and clip files of our respective newspapers, *The Plain Dealer* and the *Akron Beacon Journal,* were key factors in our research. Our heartfelt thanks to their respective staffs.

Our families proved patient during the long hours spent interviewing and writing, amid the promises of "I won't be long" as we began interviews that lasted hours, along with late-night rewriting sessions or forays into the bottomless pit of microfilm-viewing. We thank them for being with us every day, but especially for sticking with us through days like those.

Tom Feran
R. D. Heldenfels

Foreword

I first met Ernie Anderson in 1960, three years before Ghoulardi was born. We became friends immediately. Ernie Anderson personified the phrase *carpe diem.* He had the incredible ability to seize each and every day, and get the most out of it—in both work and play.

He was a very outspoken man and painfully honest when you asked him a question. Although he didn't like a whole lot of people, to me he was like the older brother I never had. During his years at Channel 8 we were practically inseparable. He was quite a character, and when he became Ghoulardi it allowed him to share with a vast TV audience the special spirit that lived within him.

What an era that was! The book you hold will give you an insight into just some of the madness that took place back then, both on and off the tube.

Ernie Anderson was the original hippie, and he influenced my life more than any other man I knew. If not for him, there would be no "Big Chuck" today. We remained good friends until he died in February 1997. I miss him very much.

I hope you enjoy this trip into the past.

Peace!

Chuck Schodowski

"Big Chuck" Schodowski

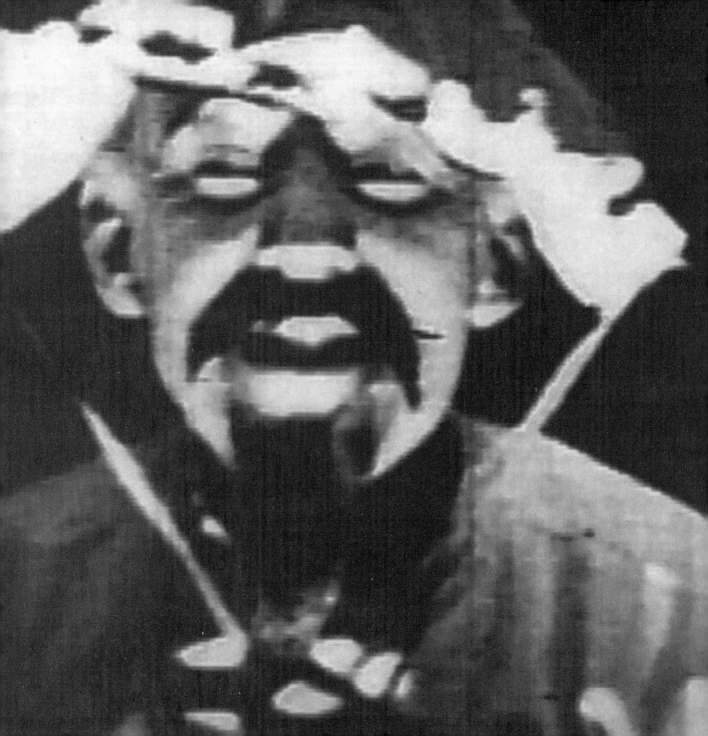

CHAPTER 1

Life Begins at 11:20

Late in 1962, in the dark depths of Cleveland's coldest and snowiest winter in 100 years, the management of Cleveland television station WJW (Channel 8) asked journeyman announcer Ernie Anderson to host a late-night horror-movie show planned for early in the new year . . .

God, No!

thought the thirty-nine-year-old veteran of a checkered career in radio and TV. Comfortable in his staff job, he had lucrative side gigs as an on-camera spokesman for Ohio Bell Telephone and other companies, and he still entertained dreams of being an actor.

He later would say he didn't mind going on camera because of the performing opportunity and the extra money—about sixty dollars a week to start. Still, he knew that his more prestigious work could dry up if he became too closely associated with the likes of *The Leech Woman*.

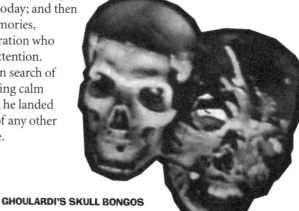

So he put on a fake mustache and beard, adopted a weird voice, and took on an assumed name: Ghoulardi.

Almost instantly the persona became more famous than the man cracking wise behind it. Adults shared his comments at work the following Monday, some shaking their heads in dismay. Newspaper columnists took sides—for and, more often, against him. Kids treated him like God, his face lodged in their minds, his hip lines becoming playground mainstays. Some left reel-to-reel audio tape recorders rolling during his show to capture the moments; they still cherish these precious bits more than thirty years later.

WJW had launched the show as, both literally and figuratively, a shot in the dark, hoping it might draw a bit of attention and a few more viewers at a time when the station ranked third (and last) in local ratings. They created an icon of popular culture whose legacy, decades later, would defy the disposable standards of modern media.

Television was growing, still rough around the edges, into the common thread of community consciousness. Ghoulardi would first conquer it, amassing an audience of a size unimaginable today; and then transcend it, surviving in the memories, attitudes, and language of a generation who would carry him to even wider attention.

In a self-doubting city ever in search of an identity, and in the unsuspecting calm before the storm of Beatlemania, he landed with an impact surpassing that of any other local broadcaster, before or since.

GHOULARDI

Chapter 1

GHOULARDI'S SKULL BONGOS

The magic began, in that winter of the century, on Friday nights at 11:20, in the old Channel 8 studios at Playhouse Square on Euclid Avenue.

City Camera news would be winding down and Ernie Anderson would just be cranking up. Most likely, he was at the Seagram Bar, informally known as "the Swamp," finishing off a Ballantine Ale and a cheeseburger; or at Pierre's, sipping martinis and playing dominoes with Pat the bartender, watching the clock as well as the game. He usually waited until the last possible moment and then had to hurry to work.

As the *Shock Theater* logo appeared on TV screens across Northeast Ohio, viewers heard strains of Ghoulardi's theme song, a Duane Eddy B-side called "Desert Rat." As the song rang through the hallways of Channel 8, Ernie's footsteps thundered an accompaniment. He grabbed the gear laid out by his teenage gofer Ron Sweed—a mustache, beard, fright wig, and glasses with only one lens—and transformed himself while still in motion, hitting the door of the studio at a dead run and almost sliding out of range as he zoomed in front of the camera. *What's tonight's movie?* he might wonder, then, *Bleep it. Doesn't matter.*

He now perched on a stool, a light at his feet casting eerie shadows on his Ghoulardi face, the omnipresent smoke in hand—a Philip Morris cigarette, sometimes in a holder; occasionally a cigar—and began to speak in a voice combining a hint of Bela Lugosi with liberal doses of hepcat—*man*, *baby*, *diggin'* and the all-purpose *group* or *groups*, as in

TOP, BOTTOM: ERNIE PREPARING FOR GHOULARDI.

"Hey, groups, we're gonna have fun tonight..."

He would not promise a great movie. It was a point of personal pride to assure the audience that the movie was bad, spectacularly so, even when it wasn't. Whether the feature was *The House on Haunted Hill* or *Attack of the Crab Monsters*, a grade-B effort or something tumbling to Z, or not even a movie at all (sometimes old TV shows were substituted), it would be mocked by Ghoulardi.

While hundreds of thousands watched Ghoulardi in Northeast Ohio, the late-night studio audience was much smaller, occasionally including a few teenage fans. Off-camera, Sweed would be helping out (and soaking up

GHOULARDI
**Life Begins
at 11:20**

information he would use years later, as the Ghoul). Sometimes an old friend of Ernie's dropped by, like actor Tim Conway, on a return visit from Hollywood, or local acquaintances like Bill "Smoochie" Gordon from WEWS (Channel 5) and KYW radio deejay Jay Lawrence. Jack Riley, another buddy, then on WERE radio, might be on hand—or on the phone from his Lakewood home, trying to satisfy Ernie's pleas for jokes.

There was a director—Ken Clark the first year, but over time whoever was on shift for the telecast, Ernie later said—and one or two cameramen, who could draw

GHOULARDI ON THE SATURDAY SET.

Ghoulardi's derision. On the air, if there was a foul-up, Ghoulardi snapped "Can't you take a picture? Dummy!" at the cameraman. It was supposed to be a joke, and off the air, demeaning comments were sometimes lightened by his admission that the technicians, too, were part of the Ghoulardi team. One cameraman, Don Quigley, Ernie delighted in tormenting on air and off, according to Ron Sweed; Ernie would set up Quigley for a small electric shock, or blast him in the face with a squirt gun during the telecast.

The inner circle consisted of three men: Ernie, his sound man and sounding board Chuck Schodowski, and projectionist/editor Bob Soinski. The job of the latter two was to organize the chaos around Ernie, to figure out where to drop joking film clips into the movies—in fact, to find the clips, not to mention the music that would become as familiar to fans as the pictures. They were also involved with the filmed sketches in which Ernie starred (and Chuck sometimes co-starred) and—a high honor from Ernie—the butt of his practical jokes.

GHOULARDI, CHUCK SCHODOWSKI IN THE PITCHING COACH SKIT.

As Ghoulardi talked to one camera, a second focused on a nearby table which held a model to be blown up with a firecracker—sometimes a car, an airplane, the new Revell line of Beatles (action figures only because Ernie gleefully sent their parts flying), or an unknown construction of a viewer's own devising. There was also a cutout of talk-show host Mike Douglas punctured with dart holes, with still more punctures likely. On Fridays, there wasn't much more visible; the Saturday and weekday shows had a complete, and constantly growing, set.

Besides the night's movie, another film often waited for telecast: a public appearance by the Ghoulardi All-Stars, the traveling softball-basketball-football team that was Ernie's pride. The movies of the team playing local schools, community groups, and other celebrity

stay

teams were a favorite with audiences as viewers recognized themselves in the crowds at the games.

Ghoulardi's monologues during and between the movies consisted of rambling jokes about local matters, staccato bursts of catchphrases— "stay sick," "turn blue," "purple knif," "cool it with the boom-booms"—or a shot at his target *du jour*. That could be the legendary local broadcaster Dorothy Fuldheim from Channel 5, or Cleveland's mayor, Ralph Locher, a charisma-free placeholder sandwiched between the beloved Anthony Celebrezze and the groundbreaking Carl Stokes. Sometimes the target was closer to home; in one surviving clip of Ghoulardi in action, a flatulent noise off-camera prompted Ernie to say, "Howard Hoffmann is not well"—an allusion to Channel 8's weatherman.

The show could also bring a new install-ment of "Parma Place," the bizarre soap opera that raised mockery of Cleveland's Poles to a new level, or some other sketch that had caught Ernie's fancy, like an eighteen-minute parody of *Gunsmoke* noteworthy mainly for being unconscionably long. (When Schodowski urged Ernie to trim it, Ernie replied that the mind-numbing length was the whole point.) Or would offer a film of one of his pantomime performances, as a hapless bowler or a man on a progressively disastrous date. Then, antagonizing management once again, Ernie could decide it was a good time to give out an execu-tive's home telephone number.

With seeming ease, he leapt into the movie, joining a herd of victims at a monster's feet;

LEFT: GHOULARDI ALL-STARS IN BASEBALL GARB. STANDING: CHUCK SCHODOWSKI (LEFT) RON SWEED (PARTLY HIDDEN), RALPH GERTZ, RAY (FRANZ THE TOYMAKER) STAWIARSKI, "POPS" TARSITANO, MICKEY FIRESTONE, WALT SARGI, MIKE LUTTON, DON NEUMEISTER, DOM LALLI, JACK MOFFITT, DICK LORIUS. KNEELING: MIKE WAGNER (LEFT) DICK GODDARD, ERNIE ANDERSON, CARL SZUBSKI, RALPH TARSITANO, BOB KASARDA, BOB (HOOLIHAN) WELLS.

sick!

GHOULARDi
Life Begins
at 11:20

17

placid among the terrified, Ghoulardi raised his hand to ask to go to the bathroom. Just as casually, he slipped in a line—"My favorite game is poker . . . You get a girl and you poke 'er"—meant to make adult viewers choke on their late-night snacks. He got away with that line, by the way, but something was always bound to happen that left his bosses apoplectic; Ernie's chat with management was a Monday-morning ritual.

The fun lasted a little over an hour and a half. There was less here than memory suggests: the movies usually filled about seventy percent of the time, and there had to be room for commercials. Some of Ghoulardi's tricks had been done before, by other hosts in other cities. But not, for the most part, in Cleveland. The movies are less prominent in fans' memories than the Ghoulardi moments forming a seamless loop of pleasure.

Some viewers were shocked. They wanted Ghoulardi stamped out, and they caused weekly trouble for the host and his associates until the day Ernie hung up his lab coat.

Others, though—the viewing majority—loved Ghoulardi. They were kids and adults, black and white, blue-collar workers sitting at home, and night owls in bars who correctly sensed in Ghoulardi a kindred spirit. All thought he was funny, some thought he was hip, in time many considered him profoundly influential. That reaction would baffle Ernie. But not us. Because the story of Ghoulardi is not just about a horror host: it's about Cleveland in the '60s, and our deep ties to television, and a man who was able to be himself while hiding behind a costume and an assumed name.

SHOWTIME, THE CLEVELAND PRESS TV MAGAZINE.

turn blue!

GHOULARDI

Chapter 1

The Life Story of Ghoulardi

GHOULARDI'S MAIL INCLUDED ELABORATE BOOK AND MAGAZINE PARODIES WRITTEN AND DRAWN BY FANS. SOME IMAGINED HIS LIFE, FRAMING THIS COMPOSITE BIOGRAPHY:

Ghoulardi attended grammar ghoul and high ghoul, where he studied alghoulbra and ghoul-ometry. He graduated magna ghoul laude.

His father warned him not to go out in the rain without his ghoulashes.

Ghoulardi loved sports. His favorite ballplayer was Ghoul Hodges, and his favorite football team was the Philadelphia Eaghouls. He liked watching them reach the ghoulposts.

Ghoulardi's mother left home, leaving his father with nothing but fangs

for the memories. Ghoulardi's father said she was nothing but a ghouldigger. Ghoulardi suffered greatly and developed a ghoult complex.

He entered show business. His debut on Lake Erie was so successful that Ghoulardi was held under for two weeks. Women said he was another Ghoul Brynner.

He did commercials for Ghoul cigarettes and ghoul-filtered Tareytons.

His favorite songs are "K-ni-fu-li, K-ni-fu-la" and "Mack the Knif."

His favorite cartoon is Ghoulwinkle.

His favorite books are The Tragedy of Ghoulius Caesar, Romeo and Ghouliet, Ghouldilocks and the Three Knifs, and Huckleberry Fink.

CHAPTER 2

The Man Who Would Be Ghoulardi

By the time he became Ghoulardi in 1963, Ernie Anderson had survived a career that would have defeated many another performer . . .

CHILDHOOD PICTURE OF ERNIE, 1925.

Born in Massachusetts on November 22, 1923, Ernie grew up in the Boston suburbs of Lynn and Lawrence, the son of a telephone installer. As late as 1993, in an interview with the *Akron Beacon Journal*'s Bob Dyer, Ernie talked about how he still loved Boston, how he felt it had a provincial quality that belied its big-city appearance. While he would love the high life that came with success, Ernie always disdained pretense, a quality that fit both his New England upbringing and the later Midwestern sensibility that would eventually lead to his first great burst of fame in Cleveland.

As a youth, he did not entertain big dreams of being a performer. He participated in high-school dramatics but realized, at a very early age, that the basic skill of memorizing lines would come hard.

"I did a little thing in a church," he said. "It was five lines. And I'm seven years old and I couldn't remember the five lines. My father sent me to—elocution, they used to call it—an elocution teacher, and I had to learn 'Casey at the Bat.' Not a chance. Not a prayer."

When Ernie did skits, it was evident that he was approximating lines; when he and Tim Conway did their comedy routines, Ernie had a script firmly in front of him, no matter how often they'd done the bit, while Conway worked from memory. Indeed, the Ghoulardi skits that best display Ernie's performing skills are silent, sparing him any effort other than a reasonably skilled pantomime.

Before Ernie had to settle on a career, there was the little matter of World War II. He joined the navy. ("I didn't want to be drafted into the army.") Working as an aircraft mechanic, he would also "fart around in show business."

Ernie joined the drum and bugle corps with his friend George Savalas (brother of actor Telly) "so we wouldn't have to stand in the chow line. We had these little passes that said we had to go to rehearsal . . . and that got us to the front of the line." While stationed in Hawaii and Guam, he also had a dance band, ran a beer garden, and showed movies at an outdoor lot.

After the war, Ernie at first thought of going to law school and spent two years at Boston's Suffolk University preparing. One day a professor who had

"I couldn't remember the five lines."

worked in radio suggested that field might be the one for Ernie, and the idea stuck with him.

He decided to take the summer off from college and support himself during that time with a summer job in radio until returning to law school in the fall.

With no radio training, but with a good voice, Ernie landed a job at a station in Montpelier, Vermont, WSKI. The call letters were supposed to make people thinking of skiing, but Ernie gleefully noted that everyone pronounced them to sound like "whiskey." Still, he said, "The minute I got into it, I said, 'I can do this. I know I can do this. I don't know if I can be a lawyer.'"

"This" was not just a matter of playing records, although Ernie enjoyed that, especially in the great pop era before the rise of rock and roll. (Depending on the interview, Ernie hated either most rock and roll or all of it.) His taste ran toward the intersection of pop, jazz, and blues; in his later years his friends included jazz musicians like trumpeter Jack Sheldon and he'd frequent jazz clubs.

People like Ernie came to radio announcing because they could create personalities. For Ernie, who would later find the Ghoulardi guise liberating, radio provided distance from the audience; it was a faceless medium in which your voice alone let you be anyone you wanted. (Many voice artists have what's known as "a face for radio.") Ernie heard what others' voices could do. He particularly admired Martin Block, who had begun spinning records on his Make-Believe Ballroom in New York City in the '30s, Bob Clayton in Boston, and radio humorists Bob and Ray.

But the giant in postwar radio, and later television, was Arthur Godfrey, a seemingly folksy, mercurial announcer and disc jockey who had taken the country by storm since joining CBS before World War II; at one point, broadcasting historian Laurence Bergreen has written, Godfrey shows accounted for twelve percent of CBS's total revenues.

Another radio pro, Fred Allen, called Godfrey "the man with the barefoot voice," and he played the man of the people to a T. But being of the people meant not being of the big companies behind broadcasting and its commercials, and Godfrey went after them.

Although some Ghoulardi fans like to credit Ernie with bringing iconoclasm to TV and radio, Godfrey displayed rough honesty years earlier. In one memorable spot, he touted a sponsor's chicken noodle soup: "There's plenty of noodles in there. And there's chicken there, too. You won't find it, but it's there . . . You find any,

ERNIE, DRESSED UP FOR A CHANGE BUT STILL FOOLING AROUND.

bring it to us." In the same spot he spooned through a bowl, showing off the noodles, wondering where the chicken was.

In a more emotional shared moment with his fans, as Godfrey broadcast the funeral of President Franklin D. Roosevelt, he sobbed audibly. And once, in a fit of pique, he fired a singer from his show—on the air. Whatever emotional turmoil afflicted Godfrey, it could spill out.

Like anyone who worked in radio in the 1940s and '50s, Ernie knew Godfrey's work. He would later say that, after listening to a recording of Godfrey, "I realized I had done pretty much the same thing Arthur Godfrey did." Perhaps like Godfrey, Ernie liked radio because "I could say anything I wanted to say."

Unlike the great and powerful Godfrey, though, up-and-coming Ernie Anderson would have to pay a price for offhandedness and irreverence.

He learned a lot in a decade in radio. Most important, he learned how to use his voice. "I worked very hard to get rid of a terrible Boston accent," he said. Then, "I found by listening to myself, I could learn microphone technique and make myself sound like I wanted to sound—lower my voice, round it out, make it more resonant, or eager, warmer, richer, harder, meaner." While he sometimes downplayed his skill—or attributed it to his terrible smoking habit—in the second half of his life it would make him rich.

ERNIE, THEN A DISC JOCKEY AT WHK RADIO, GETS A SMOOCH FROM KAY CROBAUGH AFTER WINNING A 1958 "PERSONALITY MOTOR BOAT RACE" AT THE FOREST CITY YACHT CLUB.

One thing he did not learn, though, was how to keep a job. He was fired in Montpelier for making fun of a sponsor who was in a barbershop quartet. He was fired in Providence, Rhode Island, for riding a motorcycle inside a radio station. In 1958, he came to Cleveland to work for radio station WHK, and within a year he was fired from there, too.

Ernie, who enjoyed telling and retelling stories of his station firings, sometimes said he flipped off the WHK general manager at a Christmas party and was fired on the spot. A more accurate version, also told by Ernie, is that the station gave up old-time pop music and personalities for a hard-edged, fast-talking format known as "Color Radio." Ernie hated it and was not displeased when WHK bought him out of his contract in the spring of 1959.

Still, he had to make a living, and it was tough going for a while. While trying to establish himself in voice work in commercials, he did pickup radio jobs filling in for vacationing deejays, even driving east along Lake Erie to Conneaut, some eighty miles from Cleveland near the Pennsylvania border, for one. Finally a job came up in Philadelphia, as a morning radio personality. But just before he took it, another offer came, from a Cleveland TV station. Ernie had been making $400 a week at WHK. The TV station, Westinghouse-owned KYW (Channel 3), was offering $97. He took the TV job.

"I'm not a gypsy at heart," he later said.

"I would still be at any station I had ever worked at had they not fired me . . .

ERNIE'S OFFICAL PUBLICITY PHOTO, INSCRIBED TO RON SWEED.

that's my nature." There was also a chance at performing on television, though at first his voice, not his face, was his calling card.

He began with the most boring job a voice man could have had: booth announcer. "You sit in a booth while everything else goes on," he said, "and when the end of the hour comes, you say, 'Channel 3, Cleveland.' And then you sit back and read some more and whatever, and then on the half hour, you go, 'Channel 3, Cleveland. KYW, TV-3, Cleveland.' And you do that for eight hours." (Stations eventually began taping the announcements instead of using announcers on the spot.)

Ernie was good at announcing, as surviving fragments of his '60s work indicate. A couple of promotional spots he did for movies, one for a week of suspense thrillers, the other for a series of movies "for the ladies" starring famous leading men, show the subtlety of his instrument.

The voice is the same in the two spots, but Ernie subtly changes his tone, register, and nuance to match the material. The thriller spot carries a hint of excitement and peril (heightened by the picture showing Ernie in an hourglass, slipping down with the sand). The romance spot has an air of seduction which helps make clear why stories about Ernie often include a beautiful woman nearby. (It foreshadows his commercial work years later, when he added layers of meaning to the declaration that Cougar was "the *man's* car" and insinuatingly promoted "The *Lu-u-uhv* Boat.")

GHOULARDI
The Man Who Would Be Ghoulardi

25

Announcing and promotional spots wouldn't satisfy Ernie at this point in his career as anything more than a stopgap, though. He wanted to make good in Cleveland. Successful in each of his previous radio jobs (before he lost them), Ernie burned with frustration over being dismissed at WHK before he could prove himself; he was looking for a way to prove he could be top dog in Cleveland, and wasn't too picky about whom he would have to bite to do it.

By this time, a close group of associates, most of them younger by a decade, had begun to form around Ernie. While he might have been a family man and veteran on a career track, they were drawn more by his innate sense of fun and daring, and by a style that was as casual as his preferred attire. He wore a jacket and tie when on-air duties demanded it during the workweek, but might offset them with casual slacks, desert boots, or polo shirts. On Saturdays, film editor Bob Soinski remembered, "He'd come to work maybe in a sweatshirt and blue jeans, and I thought, oh, my gosh. Everyone wore dress pants and sports shirts, not sweatshirts."

While at WHK, Ernie had become friends with a radio writer and performer named Jack Riley. (Riley later became famous as Mr. Carlin on *The Bob Newhart Show* and still shows up in high-rent TV districts like *Seinfeld* and Jay Leno's *Tonight* show—one Leno sketch had Riley playing the head of the breakaway "Republic of Cleveland.") Though Riley would be in and out of Cleveland during Ernie's era—leaving to work in New York, then returning to hone his radio skills in Cleveland, then heading off to Hollywood during the Ghoulardi years—they remained close until Ernie's death.

JACK RILEY, CA. 1967.

Another friend was Chuck Schodowski, who met Ernie as a young summer replacement engineer at KYW. Schodowski moved in 1960 to WJW, where the friendship would deepen and evolve into the professional collaboration that altered their lives.

TOP:
EARLY PHOTO OF CHUCK
SCHODOWSKI AT WJW.

BOTTOM:
ERNIE AND TIM CONWAY IN
THE "INDIAN GUIDE" SKIT.

But Ernie's friendship and collaboration with Tom Conway, a kid in his twenties from the Cleveland suburb of Chagrin Falls, began almost immediately. Later known as Tim in Hollywood, to avoid confusion with another actor, Conway had replaced Riley as a writer at KYW when Riley left for military service in 1959. He thinks it was around 1960 when he first met Ernie—but he remembers the scene precisely.

"I was driving down Euclid Avenue at about 2:00 in the morning after leaving the

GHOULARDi
Chapter 2

[TV] station, and I had blown the second, third, and fourth gears in my Karmann Ghia, so I was driving in first gear," he said. "And it sounded like an airplane going down the street, obviously. And Ernie pulled up alongside me in his car, and he rolled down his window, and said, 'Hey, a--hole, are you charging your battery?' For some reason we became friends after that."

Conway well knows the reason: both he and Ernie had a skeptical, whimsical way of looking at life in which nothing is to be taken too seriously. Conway was born half a continent away from Ernie, but what Conway calls Midwestern humor certainly fit what Ernie did, and would do. It is a humor of mockery, but without viciousness. ("I don't draw blood," Ernie said in a 1990 interview—though some of his targets would disagree.)

"There's a certain kindness to Midwestern humor that you don't have in New York or Los Angeles," said Conway. "New York can be very cruel in a sense, and Los Angeles humor is probably very chi-chi, very upperclass, very political—all of that. In the Midwest, you make fun of the people next door, the farmers, really down-home life. We were brought up with it, we understood it, we knew what was funny to people. . . . We would demonstrate to an audience things that an audience had either done or seen, or where they could say to themselves, 'Gee, I know a person like that.'"

Both men had already made moves into comedy, Ernie on radio and Conway in bits he was beginning to write for TV. In time they would be so close, "he and I were together eighteen, twenty hours a day," Conway said.

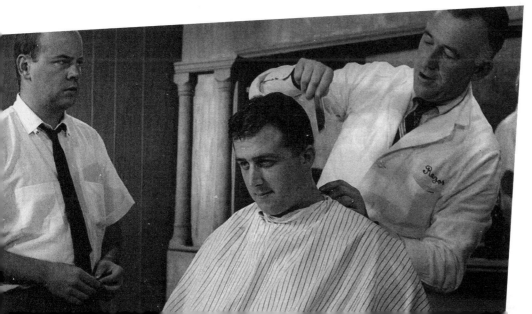

ERNIE'S 1965 TV SPECIAL: TIM CONWAY, LEFT, BROWNS PLAYER GARY COLLINS, ERNIE.

GHOULARDI
The Man Who Would Be Ghoulardi

ERNIE AND CHUCK SCHODOWSKI ON THE LINKS.

And they could give outsiders a hard time. Ann Elder, later an actress (*Laugh-In*) and comedy writer, was a twenty-year-old copywriter for Allied Advertising in Cleveland when she was sent once to direct Conway and Ernie in a commercial she had written. She asked them to do the commercial over and over; they had her kicked out of the recording session.

In bars, Schodowski recalled, fans would offer to buy Ernie a drink; Ernie would beg off, saying he was busy, then scrape part of the fan's money off the bar to buy himself a drink later. Nor was it easy to be his friend. After he moved to Hollywood, he'd forget what time it was in Ohio and wake his friend Schodowski with 4:00 a.m. calls. Rita Vennari, Ernie's devoted commercial agent in Hollywood, said he would often badger women to see if he could make them cry; if they didn't, or if they did but still managed to hold their own against him (as Vennari did), they were all right.

"He just totally lived according to whatever came out of his mind," said Woody Fraser, the television producer and former Clevelander who counted himself among Ernie's friends. "He wasn't going to put on airs for anybody or anything. If he didn't get the job, he didn't get the job. If you didn't like him, you didn't like him. And if he liked you, he was your friend for life. That's the way he was."

Ernie had a real menagerie of animals at his Willoughby home—among them a burro, a goat, and a bull, whose feeding schedules were subject to Ernie's whim. Sometimes Ernie took the livestock along on outings. On a couple of Saturdays, Ernie showed up for work and handed Bob Soinski the reins of his goat. When Ernie was done with his announcing work, he reclaimed the goat. "I don't know why he did this," Soinski said. "He never explained it." Once, when the goat was leaving a calling card of what Soinski drily called "little chocolate mothballs," Soinski firmly refused to clean it up. Ernie matter-of-factly, and barehanded, picked up the goat droppings and tossed them into a garbage can.

Something as simple as a golf outing could turn into an adventure with

GHOULARDI
Chapter 2

these guys. Schodowski went golfing once with Conway and Ernie when Ernie, a far better athlete in his own mind than in actuality, took a 27 on one hole, sending putt after putt past the cup. Enraged, Ernie drove a ball that hooked off the course, across the street, and into a man mowing his lawn. The man crossed over to the course; Schodowski prepared to calm him down only to turn and see Ernie and Conway "running away and laughing like hell." Schodowski joined his friends, the aggrieved man still in pursuit, until "we sort of got ahead of him and hid in this thicket. This guy's up there by the trees and he's all out of breath and he's swearing and he's walking and he's going to walk past us. And I think, good, it's all over."

At which point Conway jumped out of the thicket and taunted the man, starting the chase all over again. The threesome finally eluded their pursuer.

At Channel 3, while Conway's main job was writing promotional spots for upcoming programs, he also worked for Big Wilson, a radio and TV personality Conway called "the Arthur Godfrey of Cleveland." Riley, who had preceded Conway as Wilson's writer, said Wilson "was like Willard Scott before Willard Scott."

BIG WILSON

"He was this big, jolly guy," said Conway, "and he had a wife, and they just kind of talked about their personal lives—not in the way they do nowadays, it was down-home stuff." And in Wilson's prime he was a huge star. Riley recalled Wilson doing radio and TV day and night. "He was like God." He was just as imposing physically, prompting fans to greet him, "Gee, you really are big."

"I used to write little things for him," Conway said. "Most of it really came from him ... but we dropped little things for him once in a while."

Once Ernie landed at Channel 3, he and Conway began to work together—first on the station's promotional spots, in which Conway also appeared. Like most TV stations of that era, Channel 3 did a lot of local production (talk-show host Mike Douglas, later a target of Ernie's barbs, began his long-running program in Cleveland in 1961). But for Ernie and Conway, the opportunities were limited. One station executive told Conway, "You're never going to make it as talent."

The two began casting about for other opportunities. Conway and a

"And we would do it with hand puppets."

partner, Dick Moss, also took a stab at Hollywood where, Conway said, in a 1962 *Beacon Journal* interview, "after three weeks of eating mayonnaise sandwiches we decided to call it quits."

Ernie and Conway had different stories about their departure from Channel 3. According to Ernie, Channel 8 approached them about doing a presentation for advertisers in New York—showcasing movies Channel 8 planned to air that year. A Channel 8 executive liked what he saw and invited Ernie and Conway to work on a daytime movie telecast for the station—Ernie as host, Conway as director. Conway had no experience as a director, but Channel 8 bit anyway. In some tellings, Ernie said Channel 3 got wind of the presentation and fired the two. At least once he said that Conway was fired by telephone while on his honeymoon. But the two weren't worried much, because they had a job at Channel 8.

Conway's version is more complicated and not nearly as complimentary to the two performers. "We were going to come up with a show called *The Best of Paar,*" said Conway, referring to Jack Paar, host of the *Tonight* show from 1957 to 1962. "Every night, Paar would do his hour and forty-five minutes . . . and we would come on for the next fifteen minutes and do highlights of the show. And we would do it with hand puppets."

("You're kidding me," said the incredulous interviewer at this point. "Swear to God," said Conway.)

"Channel 3 said, obviously, 'you can't do this,' because Paar was on 3 and they didn't want any part of it. So we went to Channel 8 to demonstrate this thing." Channel 8 then set up a meeting with Sohio as a possible sponsor.

"We didn't have the money to have puppets, so Ernie and I pasted hair on the top of our hands, like the old Senor Wences thing. We put two eyes on our hands, and your thumb was the mouth. And we wrote fifteen minutes that we would put on for Sohio," Conway said. But they didn't actually rehearse with the puppets, an omission with painful consequences.

"They had built this little stage and we got down behind it, and had our material on a music stand. . . . Ernie had two hands above the stage, I had two hands above the stage, and we got to the bottom of the first page and realized

GHOULARDI

Chapter 2

we had no way of turning pages because our hands were occupied. I started sucking up pages with my mouth and blowing them out....

"Now, if you've ever tried holding your hands above your head for anything more than a minute, it's over. Pretty soon this pain sets in. I'm looking at Ernie and he's sweating, and now it's no longer a performance. It's, can we hold up our hands this long? About ten minutes into this, we were in so much pain, we just couldn't talk anymore. And you see these hands just kind of hanging on the stage, and just flapping up and down with hair on them."

Finally, the presentation ended. The Sohio representatives were long gone. The stagehands just wanted to clean up. Conway said he and Ernie "went to a bar and sat there, drinking beers with the hair taped to our hands and everything, trying to figure out where we went wrong."

Actually, it hadn't gone as wrong as they first thought. A Channel 8 executive saw something funny in the disaster, funny enough to offer them the movie-show job. As for Channel 3, Conway said he was about to be fired, but because Channel 3 didn't like his work, not for any perceived treachery. He quit just seconds before the hammer could fall—sitting in a manager's office on a Friday afternoon, hearing the word "you're" and calling out "I quit" before anyone could say "fired." "And Ernie quit the same day, and we went over to Channel 8 on Monday," he said.

The show they went over for was called *Ernie's Place*, but having his name in the title was no indication that Ernie had achieved any real stardom. Even after three years in Cleveland he was still "Newcomer Ernie Anderson" to Dick Shippy, the entertainment columnist for the *Akron Beacon Journal*. Shippy noted in a July 14, 1961, column that Ernie was taking over the morning-movie show on Channel 8, "hereafter to be known as 'Ernie's Place.' The 'Place' will offer live segments as well as motion picture films. Anderson comes to the station with thirteen years experience as disc jockey, announcer, actor, newscaster, and writer."

Even that suggests more planning for the show than had actually gone into it. Television in the early '60s was not that polished, and the people making a show were left on their own to do it. "Whenever we needed a prop, we'd run down to the magic shop together," said Conway. "It was that kind of arrange-ment. . . . You were completely on your own. If you needed a chair, you went and got a chair. You didn't tell somebody else to get it, because there was nobody else to go."

Some shows had more support than others—Mike Douglas, over at Channel 3, enjoyed the full backing of the station's owner, Westinghouse, which planned to syndicate his show around the country—but everyone had

TIM CONWAY "DIRECTS"
AT WJW. WITH
ENGINEERS DOM LALLI
AND JOE MARINKO.

to be ready to improvise. Douglas has often told the story of wanting a young singer named Barbra Streisand on the show for a week. Told she couldn't spend a week in Cleveland for what the show was paying, the producers found Streisand a nightclub gig in town to supplement her income.

At *Ernie's Place*, which at first ran from 9:30 to 11:00 a.m. week-days, the improvisation was even wilder. Conway was the director, but had no experience directing. "Ernie told me he wanted me as a director," said Schodowski, "that no matter what Tim does, just do it right and make it look like he was directing." Management eventually caught on, but by then Conway and Ernie were getting known as a couple of funny guys.

Conway had gone to Channel 8 so he and Ernie could work together on camera. And Ernie needed Conway on camera because the show was so lightly regarded, it couldn't get any guests. Conway accordingly began playing the guests, who boasted many occupations but a single recurring name, Dag Herferd. The name stuck well enough that the duo would use it again in the late 1960s when they made two comedy albums.

One routine featured Conway as a bullfighter. Ernie came to a break in that day's movie, the 1955 Anthony Quinn feature *The Magnificent Matador*, and said the show had a real matador on hand, "the finest matador of all time, perhaps, Mr. Dag Herferd." A portion of the interview went like this:

Tim: (My teacher) was probably one of the outstanding bullfighters of all time. He led the league in ears for five years.

Ernie: Led the league in ears? What's that?

Tim: As you destroy a bull, or kill it, you get sort of a reward. One ear would be a fairly good kill, two ears would be a good kill, two ears and a tail would be the highest accolade you could get.

Ernie: How many ears do you have, Dag?

Tim (touches each side of his head): Two.

Ernie: Bull's ears.

Tim: Well, I don't have any ears.

Ernie: You don't have any bull's ears?

Tim: I have one bull's hoof.

Ernie: Did the committee award you that . . . ?

Tim: No, the bull did.

(Ernie and Conway later reprised the bit as a tighter routine on one of their albums.)

As was so often the case with Ernie, sometimes the material pushed the limits of propriety. "I think he was like [Howard] Stern is now," said Riley. But Conway took pains to note that the restrictions on TV's content were severe, and anything he or Ernie later did was mild by modern standards.

"You had to come up with something amusing and possibly make people laugh," Conway said. "Nowadays, obviously, you just fall back and say a couple of swear words." Still, controversy occasionally came to *Ernie's Place*, as when Ernie referred to politician Richard Nixon as "Tricky Dicky" on the air. Although it was hardly the first time that Nixon had been hit with that name, viewers screamed. "Ernie was taken off the air for a week until everything cooled down," Conway said. "We just ran the movies and a slide and some news."

Ernie also pushed his luck off camera.

Ernie had a new motorcycle—the Golden Goose, a Honda with an eagle on the tank—and on his weekend shift he drove it into a back room at the station. When that went unchallenged, he began riding it in the hallways. Still no trouble, so he added riding through the newsroom. Then it started escalating.

Ernie would open the doors to news director Norm Wagy's office. Then, from Euclid Avenue, he would roar into the front door, through the lobby, through the newsroom, and into Wagy's office, make one circle around his desk, and exit through the front lobby and out of the building.

After that, he'd go do his announcing work, then at a break ride around again. But even people who saw him make his rides through the halls were astounded one day when they found a tire mark going up the walls of Wagy's office.

A memo came out the following Thursday: "Please do not ride your motorcycle through the lobby or Norm Wagy's office anymore."

On the show, Ernie and Conway were having a great time, if not the most artistically elevated one. A big problem was that Conway did not know how to "back-time" the movies, making sure the comedy bits were short enough for all of the movie to fit the time slot. Too often, the show ended before the movie. "People would get a little p---ed off when we did *Citizen Kane* because they wouldn't see Rosebud," said Conway. Soon they were "burning" the film, Schodowski said—running the movie through commercial breaks, unseen

ERNIE AND TIM CONWAY GO FOR THE GOLD IN GO-KARTS DURING A BREAK FROM *ERNIE'S PLACE*.

GHOULARDi
The Man Who Would
Be Ghoulardi

by viewers. "You miss a lot of the movie. And even so, at the end, we still didn't have time to show all the film."

Finally, they started running the ends of the unfinished movies on the Friday show. "It got to be kind of an inside thing, that 'these guys don't know what the hell they're doing,'" said Conway, "and it was obvious on the air that we didn't know what we were doing, and people just thought that was hysterical."

How hysterical had become evident by September of 1961. The half hour preceding *Ernie's Place* had been filled by an exercise show hosted by Ed Allen, but when Channel 8's contract with Allen ended, *Ernie's Place* was expanded into Allen's slot.

It was about that time that Rose Marie came to Cleveland.

"I was in town doing a promotion for the first year of *The Dick Van Dyke Show*," said the actress, who played comedy writer Sally Rogers on the show. "You know, 'Be sure to watch on Channel 8!' This director was throwing funny lines at me. I said, 'Who is that guy? I want to meet him.'"

The guy was Conway, who told her that he and Ernie had worked up "a lot of funny stuff." She said, "I wanted to see it. They didn't have any film, so I listened to an audiotape of a baseball game that was rained out, and they were the announcers trying to stretch. Very funny.

"I never did anything like this before, but I took it to Steve Allen. Steve said, 'What are you doing? When did you become an agent?'"

But Allen listened, and was intrigued enough to take a look at some hastily shot videotape. He considered Conway "richly, hysterically funny, before he even opened his mouth."

"To this day," Allen wrote in his 1982 book *More Funny People*, "I've never seen more than the first two minutes of it, because it took me only about thirty seconds to realize that Rose Marie had been absolutely right."

Ernie, unfortunately, was the straight man—the role Allen played in sketches on his show. Conway was invited west; Ernie was not.

Rose Marie, who became Conway's manager for about two years, said, "I felt terrible about breaking up the team."

Conway did not leave town permanently after the first time he did the Allen show, choosing to go back and forth when Allen called, still living in Chagrin Falls. And he did not really want to leave. "I was having that good a time in Cleveland, with Ernie," he said. "I also thought, 'Steve Allen, that's the end.' When he did the *Tonight* show, with those three guys on the street—you know, Don Knotts, Louis Nye, Tom Poston—to me that was as good as television gets. So if you get on Steve Allen, what else is left?"

ERNIE'S PLACE, THE SHOW ERNIE HAD BEFORE GHOULARDI. ERNIE, LEFT, WITH READING EXPERT R. BUCHANAN ADAMS.

The show "went in the toilet."

For Conway, there was an offer to work with Oscar-winning actor Ernest Borgnine on a new situation comedy, *McHale's Navy*, which had begun preparations for its premiere in the fall of 1962. (It would run for four seasons.) Still, Conway wasn't sure, and shared his uncertainty with the station manager at Channel 8, who said, "Well, maybe this will help you: you're fired. If you don't go out [to Hollywood], you're nuts. So you're fired." Conway then went west with the TV navy and Ernie tried to soldier on in Cleveland.

Ernie's Place did not even survive Conway's first burst of success. With Conway commuting to performances out west, Ernie said in the *Monsterscene* interview, the show "went in the toilet. . . . Without Tim it wasn't fun anymore. I did straight interviews with guys who were as boring as whale [bleep]."

Indeed, there is film of an interview Ernie did in 1961 with Andy Griffith, who was promoting the second season of *The Andy Griffith Show*. Ernie seems comfortable enough, though to Griffith's visible irritation he is also unprepared: he credits Griffith with a record someone else did, and is unaware why Griffith is in Cleveland.

Conway also suspects that, without his buddy around, Ernie just didn't have the confidence to do the show on his own, a reasonable assertion given the way Ernie regularly surrounded himself with helpmates and co-stars. To Ernie's relief, *Ernie's Place* made its last appearance in January 1962.

To his financial comfort, Ernie's voiceover and on-camera commercial work was picking up. He was becoming the top voice in Cleveland, and over the years he would star in commercials for Ohio Bell, Millbrook Bread (its "reusable, reclosable, plastic bag" was a major selling point in those days), Star muffler shops, and other sponsors.

But there was still that urge to perform, to be something other than a pitchman—to let loose the Ernie Anderson who had flourished on radio station after radio station until things went awry. He hungered to perform. Even the credit list on a movie announcement would turn into a comedy, as Ernie added made-up names or those of Channel 8 employees to the credits.

He never heard a complaint, because he made the absurd credits sound so real.

Ernie briefly played the sidekick to Dale Young, who had a daytime show on Channel 8 beginning on October 1, 1962. Meant to take advantage of the audience Mike Douglas on Channel 3 and the older *1 O'Clock Club* on Channel 5 had found in the daytime, the show lasted only a little more than six months. By the time it was cancelled, though, in April 1963, Ernie had found his true calling.

He sometimes made it sound offhand. "I was doing a Christmas show," he said, referring to a taping of the station employees and their families, which Channel 8 televised Christmas morning as a sort of thank-you to its staff. "I sort of emceed it. And that morning, when we were through, a guy named Bob Buchanan [the Channel 8 station manager] came up and said, 'We just bought twenty-six—or whatever it was—horror movies. And we're gonna play 'em Friday night and we need a host.' I had just hosted this thing and I guess he was kind of impressed. Otherwise he had no motivation to pick me out of the mob."

While Ernie might have been approached at the taping, it's hard to believe that performance alone got him the movie-hosting job. He had by then worked on the air for Channel 8 on *Ernie's Place* and was being seen and heard in commercials around town. Whatever the reason for choosing him, though, Ernie was given an incredible opportunity. Although he might not have picked a late-night horror show as his venue, once the choice was made for him, Ernie found a format in which all his favorite qualities were set free.

How that format came into being is another story, one that has been overlooked for more than thirty years. It begins, not with Ernie, but with an aspiring makeup artist, a Cleveland restaurant, and a novel idea.

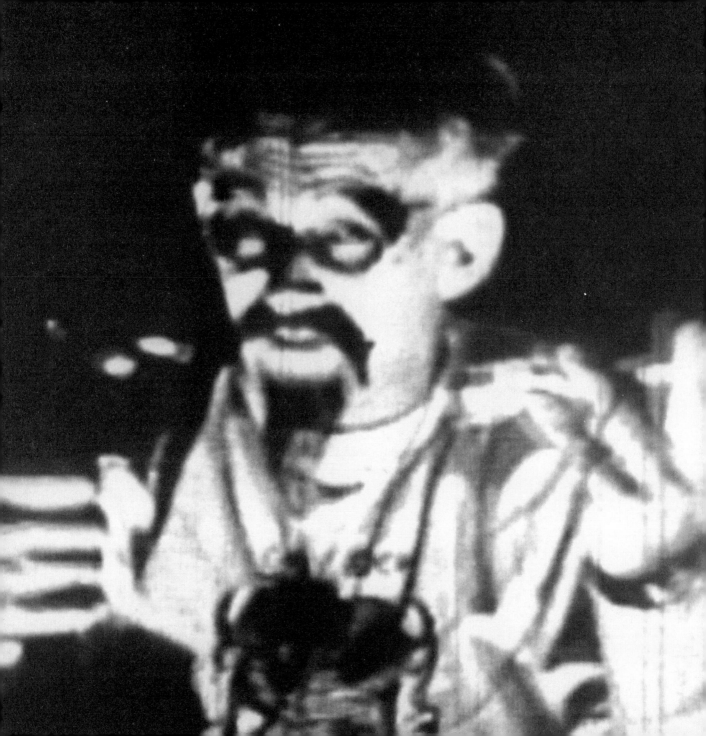

CHAPTER 3

What Is This Thing Called Ghoulardi?

Ralph Gulko was night manager at the Tasty Shop on Euclid Avenue when he heard that WJW was thinking of putting on a late-night horror-movie show . . .

The notion intrigued Gulko, who had been working the previous eighteen months in the restaurant business but harbored ambitions of becoming a theatrical makeup artist.

He had been playing around with makeup since high school, had received professional training in the armed forces as a macrofacial prosthetist—dealing with burn cases and accident victims—and had taken training on the movie *The Alamo* while still on active duty in San Antonio, Texas. Now back home in Cleveland, he was working on obtaining his Ohio cosmetology license.

WJW employees were regular patrons of the nearby Tasty Shop, and Gulko had become friendly with many, including Howard Hoffmann, announcer and weatherman, and Sheldon Saltman, the station's promotion manager and master of ballyhoo. He had heard Shelley Saltman and station manager Bob Buchanan talking about a plan—based on an idea Saltman remembered from a Boston station—of having their new horror-movie show hosted by an appropriately themed character.

Gulko immediately thought of a character he had been using for fun at Halloween, a character unlike any he had seen on television. He also thought of Hoffmann, who had been best man at Gulko's wedding, and—prior to joining WJW—one of the four singing Men of Texaco who introduced Milton Berle on his *Texaco Star Theatre.* Hoffmann was, in fact, a likely candidate for the movie job because of his extensive on-air experience.

Gulko worked up some presentation sketches for his character, featuring a look in which the makeup was very clean, without the pallor, dark eye circles, and more elaborate makeup already associated with other horror-movie hosts. He also came up with four possible names for the character: Chaim A. Ghoul, Dr. Ghoulkoff, Professor Ghoulski, and Ghoulardo. "Everything was a takeoff on my name," he said. "I was going with the 'ghoul' type sound."

He also intended the names to reflect the ethnic diversity of the East Side neighborhoods in which he had grown up in Cleveland: Jewish, Russian, Polish, and Italian.

"I didn't know how they were going to go [over] in the city, with so many different groups and religions. This character could be anything they wanted him to be. He could fit in anywhere," Gulko said. He played around with the idea and went back to the station within a little over twenty-four hours.

He took his concept to Saltman, who thought it was a great idea. "We were hurting," he said, "and my job was to get ratings. I was looking for a look for the station, and Ralph came to me with this idea."

Saltman carried the idea up the station food chain, ultimately to Buchanan. "I convinced them this would be perfect, and Howard would be perfect . . . . They sat down and said, 'No, Howard is not the guy—Ernie is the guy.'"

Exactly why Hoffmann was passed over is still open to speculation. Hoffmann and Saltman both acknowledge that Buchanan and Hoffmann often feuded over matters involving AFTRA, the station's performers' union. In addition, said Saltman, "They had a big contract with [Ernie] and *Ernie's Place* had bombed . . . They had to use him—they had to pay him."

The station now had a character and an actor to play him. They needed a name.

"We all started kicking around the name," said Saltman. "Nobody really thought those names would work, and so I said to Ralph, 'What do you think? We'll drop the 'o' and we'll call him Ghoulardi.'"

"Ghoulardi was terrific," Gulko said. "It had a softer sound to it than Ghoulardo."

Now to bring the public in on the game.

THE HOUSE ON HAUNTED HILL. VINCENT PRICE STARS IN THE FIRST SHOCK THEATER PRESENTATION.

The new show went on the air as <u>Shock Theater</u> on January 18, 1963.

The featured movie was *The House on Haunted Hill*, starring Vincent Price. The host, Gulko's character played by Ernie Anderson, went nameless.

Station managers knew what the name was. Gulko knew what the name was. Ernie probably knew the name, too. But viewers were left in the dark, because the station planned to hold a public contest to "name" the new show's host.

The hook was the nine-day Cleveland Boat Show, opening January 26, which annually drew more than 100,000 people.

Channel 8 set up a booth and received about 17,000 entries in its "name the host" contest—"piles upon piles of cards," Saltman said. The contest, of course, was a sham.

"We had already picked the name. What we did, we looked and saw which were the five closest to it, and everybody got a prize," said Saltman.

GHOULARDI
What Is This Thing
Called Ghoulardi?

41

"Just sit there and comment on the movie."

—WJW MANAGEMENT TO ERNIE ANDERSON

"[It was] a pseudo-contest. We weren't really fooling the public, I don't consider. What we did there was creative license."

An entrepreneur who works by the motto "You can sell anybody anything," Saltman sees such promotions as part of the TV game of the time. He well remembers other stunts, such as telling viewers they would see fifteen minutes of color TV one night, when the only existing video was black and white. All the station did was a run a black-and-white videotape so quickly that people thought they saw colors in the blurred image.

"You don't really cheat anybody," Saltman said, "and nobody gets hurt."

So by mid-February, the show had a face, a personality, and now finally a name.

Gulko remained on the scene for the first few weeks, showing Ernie how to handle the costume, how to make the beard slip and yet still stay on his face. He got paid for a few things—the makeup, the beard and mustache. But his contribution to the show would be ignored, known only to his family and a few friends, for almost thirty-five years.

The show was becoming Ernie's, and it was now being run by him and a small circle of associates.

"The first few couple of weeks, the show was really nothing," said Chuck Schodowski, who was the audio man, engineer, and, in all but title, producer and music director. "Ernie was just doing what the station wanted him to do. They were saying, 'Just sit there and comment on the movie'—because it was live, he could see the movie—'and that's it, then lead into the breaks.'"

The style was simple, even spartan. Ernie wore the raggedy mustache and Vandyke goatee prescribed by Gulko, but not yet the fright wig and lab coat that would later become familiar. He dumped an early part of the Ghoulardi look—a faucet on his forehead—because it left a large blotch that was hard to cover, even with makeup, when he did commercials as himself. (One early newspaper story had it that Ghoulardi wore a third eye, which kept falling off his forehead, though years later Ernie insisted Ghoulardi "never had three eyes.")

Only his face appeared on camera, in classic "talking head" fashion. The lighting on the set was really just one light near Ernie's feet pointed up toward his face—a spooky touch borrowed from every big brother with a flashlight who has tried to scare a younger sibling. Ernie took credit for the no-frills lighting design, telling one interviewer he "didn't want to mess with the technicians, because they're the ones that can screw up your show."

The station was comfortable with the format. Simple and cheap, it had been successful elsewhere and fit into a growing tradition.

Vampira was probably the first of the breed, according to Elena M. Watson, author of the book *Television Horror Movie Hosts.* With a slinky look reminiscent of Morticia Addams, Vampira—actually a Finnish actress named Maila Nurmi—began slithering across TV screens in Los Angeles in 1954. She employed the sort of bent humor that included telling viewers "I hope you were lucky enough to have had a horrible week" and concocting a cocktail that "will absolutely kill you." She not only hosted bad movies but actually appeared in one—*Plan 9 from Outer Space,* Ed Wood's 1959 camp classic—a practice that would be continued by later hosts such as Elvira, Mistress of the Dark (played since 1981 by actress Cassandra Peterson as a perkier and more bosomy variation on Vampira).

TV horror began to boom in 1957, when Universal Pictures sold its feature films, most notably its long line of horror movies, including the original *Frankenstein* and *Dracula,* for broadcast. In the wake of these movies came the TV hosts: Philadelphia's Roland and New York City's Zacherley (both played by the same actor, John Zacherle), Dr. Lucifer in Baltimore, Gregory Grave in Kansas City, and others. Some were trying stunts that would still be fresh to Cleveland viewers in the next decade; Zacherle, for example, inserted his image into movies he was hosting.

Cleveland got its first taste of horror celebrity in early 1958, when disc jockey Pete Myers began hosting movies on WJW. Myers was better known as "Mad Daddy," a red-hot radio deejay famous for his rapid-fire rhyming patter, trademark phrases like "wavy as gravy" and "mellow as Jell-O," and an unbridled approach to the world that astonished the seemingly daring Ernie Anderson.

In 1958, Myers wanted to jump from WJW radio, where he would be succeeded by "Casey at the Mike" Casey Kasem, to WHK—only to be stalled by a clause in his WJW contract that kept him from working for a competitor

GHOULARDI MOVIES

CREEPY CREATURES

From Hell It Came (1957). "As walking-tree movies go, this is at the top of the list."—*Leonard Maltin's 1996 Movie & Video Guide* .

Daughter of Dr. Jekyll (1957). Werewolf.

The Unknown Terror (1957). Fungus men.

Target Earth (1954). Robots from Venus.

She-Devil (1957). Witch.

The Cat Girl (1957). Woman believes her soul is in a leopard.

Kronos (1957). Hundred-foot-tall alien.

Attack of the 50 Foot Woman (1958). "Kids always talked about it after it was on, never quite sure if it was supposed to be funny or not."—Michael Weldon, *Psychotronic.*

The Man in Half-Moon Street (1944). Scientist stays young with gland transplants.

Dr. Cyclops (1940). Mad scientist—is there any other kind?—shrinks people.

Sh! The Octopus (1937). Based on a play about a gorilla. Really.

First Man into Space (1959). Mutant blood-sucking astronaut.

FROM HELL IT CAME. THE DARK SIDE OF TREE-HUGGING.

for ninety days. Not one to let the public forget him during his off-the-air exile, Myers staged a parachute jump from a Piper Cub flying 2,200 feet above Lake Erie—a Coast Guard commander said he would have stopped the jump if he had had the legal means to do so. Myers made the jump while reciting a rhyme he composed as he fell: "If you want mellow publicity [Jan Mellow was the *Cleveland News* reporter covering the story],/Bail out and win it./Though Mad Daddy's off the air,/Hang loose, Mother Goose, he's in it."

Myers was a driven man. In 1968, nine years after he left for New York to work for WNEW radio, he received the de facto demotion of being moved from an afternoon on-air shift to evenings. Soon after, just forty years old, he turned a shotgun on himself in his bathroom, leaving a suicide note that cited the program move.

"MAD DADDY" MYERS PREPARES FOR HIS BIG JUMP, 1958.

While at WHK, Ernie was Myers's twice-daily lead-in. Ernie worked from noon to 2:00 p.m. and 6:00 to 8:00 p.m.; Myers worked 2:00 to 4:00 p.m. under his own name and 8:00 to 10:00 p.m. as Mad Daddy. Ernie's success and his reputation for outrageousness would come to eclipse Myers's, and his ambition would eventually take him to Hollywood with just a few hundred bucks in his pocket. ("He'd rather take a paycheck than a chance," was a cutting judgment Ernie made of others.) But his self-proclaimed laziness and easy trust in luck kept him from sharing or even understanding his friend's consuming drive.

"You're an a--hole for doing this," Ernie later recalled telling the sky-diving Myers, in a 1984 *Cleveland Magazine* profile by writer David DeLuca. "Success didn't mean that much to me. If I had to jump out of a plane to be one, I'd pass."

But Jack Riley, who knew both Myers and Ernie, thinks it likely that Ernie was influenced by Mad Daddy's brief turn as a horror host on WJW-TV. DeLuca wrote, "Both liked the same kind of music, the weird sound effects, and the wiggy lingo." Direct comparisons to Ghoulardi are difficult, though, since Myers's work was shown live and was not preserved.

Mad Daddy's primary prop was a velvet, hooded "nightmare robe." His chief visual gimmick was an inverted close-up of his face. Don Clark, later a devoted Ghoulardi fan and chronicler known as Kaptin Ignatz, remembers watching Mad Daddy's upside-down broadcast; he asked his mother if he could overturn the TV to right the image.

Ernie might not have seen Mad Daddy on television, but he knew his radio style and was well acquainted with Mad Daddy's patter and anarchic spirit. After his initial, by-the-script debut as Ghoulardi, he started to discover the benefits of appearing on TV as someone else.

"I tried to be as crazy as I could, within the limitations they were setting up for me," he said in a 1990 *Plain Dealer* magazine interview. "After I did it the first time, the program director came down and said, 'Well, that isn't what we want.' He wrote me a script for the next week, which he put on the TelePrompTer. I read it, but I destroyed it, you know what I mean? He wanted serious. Nobody was gonna buy serious."

"Ernie said, once you hide behind the goatee and mustache, you can say outrageous things," Schodowski recalled. "His comments got more and more bizarre." For example, "no one ever, ever criticized the movie. He started criticizing the movie, and that's what really did it. He said, 'This movie is so bad, if you look real close, you can see the strings that this spaceship flies on.'" Another favorite remark: "This movie is so bad, you should just go to bed."

But it wasn't merely what Ghoulardi said that intrigued viewers. It was the way he said it.

Other horror hosts parodied the inflections of Bela Lugosi, Boris Karloff, and Vincent Price, and took their comedic cues from Bobby Pickett's 1962 novelty record "The Monster Mash." Ghoulardi was something else and something more—more beatnik than Boris and more boogie man than bogeyman.

Beneath his Ghoulardi disguise, and also beneath the business suit he wore as a commercial spokesman, Ernie was a big band and jazz fan who spoke the language of hipsters and show business. When he donned the chin whiskers of Ghoulardi, the air was thick with "cool" and "man" and "digging" and "baby," and the attitude was distinctly bohemian.

His put-on accent, sometimes inconsistent and occasionally dropped completely, was an original blend of Cleveland ethnic and a Jackie Mason–style imitation of Bela Lugosi's Dracula.

Instead of talking down to viewers or trying to act "with it," in the manner of adults hosting shows meant for teens, Ernie evolved a style of his own, with a language to go with it. His catchwords and phrases rapidly became part of the local lexicon.

There were the hipster phrases: "Turn blue," "Stay sick," and the all-purpose "Cool it"—later extended to "Cool it with the boom-booms" (for "Stop messing with the firecrackers").

"This movie is so **bad,** you should just go to bed."

"Fink" was turned backwards to the pejorative "knif"—or "purple knif," as in his catchphrase, "All the world's a purple knif."

Years before Don Adams popularized the phrase as secret agent Maxwell Smart on TV's *Get Smart,* Ghoulardi was asking viewers, "Would you beLIEVE?!"—or telling them, "This, you won't beLIEVE." Viewers were greeted as "group," and something "over there" was "ova dey!"—in the western Pennsylvania, Italian-American inflection always used by one of WJW's studio directors.

The station occasionally called his character "Ghoulardi-o," as in the old expression "daddy-o," in an attempt to show the kids in the audience it was, like, hep, man. Ernie not only resisted it, he tried to make his own change in the name.

"For whatever reason, Ernie didn't like the spelling," Schodowski said. He insisted it was "Goulardi" (no *H*), while WJW just as firmly kept the *H* in the name. Newspaper stories about the show were accordingly inconsistent about the spelling, and Ernie did nothing to help the situation, signing *H*-less autographs up until his death. (One Ghoulardi sweatshirt bears imprints of both the WJW "Ghoulardi" logo and Ernie's "Goulardi" signature.)

The confusion didn't distract the fans. Ghoulardi's irreverent monologues full of ad-libbed movie putdowns, jokes, and readings from fan and hate mail immediately became a far bigger attraction than the films they interrupted.

Channel 8 purchased the first package of horror movies for the show in late 1962, out of something close to desperation. The station, a CBS affiliate, was getting whipsawed late at night by a tandem peculiar to Cleveland. KYW, the NBC affiliate, was passing up the *Tonight* show in favor of a talk show starring former *Tonight* host Steve Allen that was syndicated by Westinghouse, the station's owner. WEWS, the ABC affiliate, was consequently able to pick up NBC's *Tonight,* hosted by newcomer Johnny Carson.

Channel 8 program manager Bob Huber hoped to make inroads on Friday night with what he called "less-than-A movies." In other words, the station did not enter the late-night war with *Gone With the Wind.*

Contrary to myth, however, the flicks weren't always that bad.

"STAY SICK"
(-NOULARDI –

Many of the movies had been made during the horror craze of the late 1950s, destined for drive-in screens and a minimally attentive audience of smooching teenagers. Because Ghoulardi made fun of them, though, they usually are remembered as grade Z.

But no less a connoisseur of schlock than Michael Weldon, publisher of *Psychotronic* magazine (which extensively chronicles horror, science fiction, fantasy, and exploitation films), contends that the movies shown on *Shock Theater* had a wider range. A Lakewood High School graduate, he remembers them firsthand as ranging "from classics to disputed bad, to the ones nobody would like."

The first *Shock Theater* feature, 1958's *The House on Haunted Hill,* starred Vincent Price as a man who offers to pay people a fortune if they spend a night in his home. (Directed by horrormeister and self-promoter William Castle, in theatrical showings the movie included one of Castle's most famous stunts: a skeleton moving along a cable over theatergoers' heads as if it had jumped from the screen.) *The 1997 Video Movie Guide* gives it three stars out of a possible five, and calls it "humorous at times, deadly serious at others." *Leonard Maltin's 1996 Movie and Cable Guide* awards it three out of four stars, and calls it "probably the Castle film which holds up best on TV." The authoritative, multivolume *Motion Picture Guide* summed it up as "silly, but good fun."

It may have been a dog, but it didn't bark.

The following week showcased *The Cosmic Man,* a 1959 feature with John Carradine as an alien bringing a message of peace to hostile earthlings. More in the remembered Ghoulardi vein, this was dismissed as a "turkey" by *Video Movie Guide* and as a "well-intentioned message . . . lost in a poorly made film" by Maltin. But a week after that, the quality rebounded with another Vincent Price feature, *The Bat,* a 1959 adaptation of the novel and play by Mary Roberts Rinehart and Avery Hopgood, which, though talky, was hardly terrible.

Kaptin Ignatz was one of the viewers who first saw Ghoulardi on the night of *The Bat.* Writing in his fans' newsletter, *Ghoul Pardi,* in 1991, Ignatz remembers Ghoulardi's shadowy face, framed by an oscillating circle of light. Even more exciting, he recalls Ghoulardi's promise to show a real dead bat on the air after the movie.

"Turned out to be a broken baseball bat," Ignatz wrote. "But as this movie was later rerun, we got to feast our hungry eyes on a real, live, small rubber novelty bat."

It was a thrill—if you were eleven.

Given the distance of time, it is hard to understand why fans thought a joke as lame as that was so great and even memorable. But the first audience for the show came to it without expectations. Ghoulardi's antics would be

GERALD HAERTER IN CALTIKI, THE IMMORTAL MONSTER (1959). IS THAT A CLEAR-BOTTOMED GHOULARDI MUG IN HIS HAND?

"Papa-Oom

MME. CURIE-OSITIES

Attack of the Crab Monsters (1957). Giant crabs created by radioactivity.

The Giant Behemoth (1959). Radioactive dinosaur.

The Atomic Submarine (1959). Sub pursues alien vessel in Arctic.

The Atomic Man (1956). Sees seven seconds into future.

The Cyclops (1957). Fifty-foot giant created by radioactivity. Michael Weldon notes that this and two other radioactive epics, *The Amazing Colossal Man* (1957) and *War of the Colossal Beast* (1959) "all feature nearly naked giant bald guys." *Cyclops* bonus: giant rats.

Them! (1954). Giant radioactive ants.

imitated, duplicated, and surpassed by later TV hosts, but in 1963, television was still like a freshly opened jar of peanut butter. The extra-super-chunky Ghoulardi opened the door to an irreverent new world.

In that context, it didn't matter if the movies were great. Like many fans, Weldon said, "I took them seriously, but I loved the way he made fun of them." Fans responded to Ernie's style, which was blossoming.

The oscillating circle of light around Ghoulardi's face was one of several innovations added by Schodowski, who began to see the show as his own electronic playground of low- and high-tech stunts.

On the low side was the telephone, which did not even ring. Ernie—never one to trust in or give a cue for a sound effect—knocked on the old-fashioned telephone that sat beside him before answering it, rather than waiting for an off-camera ring. He usually flung out its two pieces in an extravagant Ed Norton–like gesture, rocking back in his chair because "some knif is on the phone ova dey."

On the high side were the "drop-ins," film clips that were inserted absurdly into movies at moments of high horror. These were the province of Schodowski and Bob Soinski (pronounced so-IN-skee), a projectionist and film editor. Soinski started in TV during his senior year at Cathedral Latin High School in Cleveland, working part time as a film shipper, sending copies of movies and TV shows from KYW to other stations to use as part of a process known as bicycling. After graduating in 1956, he got a tryout as a film editor and was good enough to get a full-time job as an editor; in 1961, he went to WJW as an editor and projectionist, running the films the station televised.

As it became clear that Ghoulardi movies were not holy writ, Soinski began looking for ways to play with them, notably through the drop-ins.

"It just seemed to fit with the character," Soinski said. "We seemed to be on the same vibe about how the show should be. The movies were bad. The idea was, let's not defend them . . . let's have fun with them. So the idea came to me

GHOULARDI

Chapter 3

LEFT: ATTACK OF THE CRAB MONSTERS (1957)
MIDDLE: THE GIANT BEHEMOTH (1959)
RIGHT: THE CYCLOPS (1957)

Mow-Mow"

that we could interrupt the movie and flash a few things here and there.

"Say there was a scene of people dancing, and I had a clip of a fat lady dancing like a ballerina. I would think, this is a good place to interrupt the dancing, we'll just cut to the fat lady." Scenes of people boarding a train inevitably led to a clip of two trains crashing. "We'd use maybe five or six in a movie, so they weren't constantly being peppered in. But just when you'd forget about this happening, one would pop up . . .

"I think the kids liked it," Soinski said. "Some of the adults actually watched the movies and complained that we were interrupting the movie. Ernie would say, 'If you want to watch a movie, don't watch this one.'"

In his search for material, Soinski sorted through the various films that the station had bought. "They had old newsreel clips of funny people, funny things. That's where I found the 'Papa-Oom-Mow-Mow' guy."

"This guy was in a gurning contest," said Schodowski, referring to facial-contortion competition in the British Isles. "I've got a picture—this guy clearly has his lip over his nose . . . doing his 'gurning,' and I was dying laughing, and I said, 'I have the perfect piece of music for this.' And it was 'Papa-Oom-Mow-Mow.'"

Then an obscure novelty vocal recording by a Los Angeles foursome called the Rivingtons, the song was typical of the contributions Schodowski made to the show.

Schodowski would become a Northeast Ohio legend in his own right as the host of the *Big Chuck and Lil' John* show. In the early '60s, he had an engineering degree from the National Radio School (later known as the Electronics Technology Institute), had worked briefly at Channel 3, and had been an engineer at Channel 8 since 1960.

The Ghoulardi show gave him his beginning as a TV personality. Ernie's own involvement in the show "really depended on Ernie," said Schodowski, and varied from week to week. "If Ernie had an idea for something he'd work at it like a bulldog. But often he'd mostly rely on myself and Bob Soinski. And

THE FAMOUS "GURNING MAN." SING ALONG, WON'T YOU?: "PAPA-OOM-MOW-MOW . . ."

GHOULARDI MOVIES

B-MOVIE ACTORS FROM OUTER SPACE

Queen of Outer Space (1958) with Zsa Zsa Gabor.

The Cosmic Man (1959) with John Carradine.

The Brain from the Planet Arous (1958) with John Agar. "Good fun for the cult of John Agar fanatics."— *The Motion Picture Guide*

BRAIN CAPERS

The Monster and the Girl (1941). Ape with transplanted human brain.

The Brain Eaters (1958). Alien parasites take over humans. "Pretty typical stuff as 'brain' movies go."— *The Motion Picture Guide*

GHOULARDI WAS MEANT FOR ONE AS BEAUTIFUL AS YOU

Vincent Price has a special place in Ghoulardi history, appearing in the show's first movie, *The House on Haunted Hill* (1958); the first one televised in color, *House of Wax* (1953); and one of the most memorable, *The Bat* (1959).

we were mostly having fun." As Soinski rummaged around for film clips, Schodowski brought in other elements, starting with the music.

Ernie disdained rock and roll. Schodowski was fond of polkas—the only music he knew when he was young—and had an acquired taste for brooding instrumentals and rhythm and blues. "I had worked in a foundry," said Schodowski, "and I was the only white guy on the night shift. I listened to Moondog"—the legendary deejay Alan Freed, who first made his name playing R & B in Cleveland. "I got all these old records and thought it was very fitting [music] for the [Ghoulardi] character."

Duane Eddy's "Desert Rat," a slow, murky piece reeking of back-alley knife fights, became the Ghoulardi theme song. Background and break selections might include Link Wray's "Rumble" or Booker T and the MGs' "Green Onions," which had been a hit the year before Ghoulardi went on the air. All were instrumentals. Schodowski's and Ernie's tastes intersected in the work of jazz organist Jimmy McGriff. He was no trailblazer—*The Illustrated Encyclopedia of Jazz* brushes him off as a mere imitator of great keyboard man Jimmy Smith—but he made some catchy recordings, among them a pounding version of Ray Charles's "I Got a Woman," which became an Ernie favorite.

Once—in one of those moments suggesting Ernie was everywhere in Cleveland in the '60s—Ernie, McGriff, and a young Clevelander named Don King came together.

King (later known for promoting—and nearly ruining—professional boxing) "owned a place way past [East] 55th Street, and he invited me up there one night . . . for a benefit," said Ernie. "I got to know him, very well as a matter of fact, and Jimmy McGriff was playing at his place. And I got to know Jimmy McGriff." The organist made a record, "Turn Blue," that took its title from the Ghoulardi catchphrase. "He did it, like, for me," said Ernie. Other musicians over the years would follow suit.

The polkas, especially prominent when ethnic Parma became a recurring show topic, included Frank Wojnarowski's "Hej Gory Moje Gory" (later released by another band as "Ghoulardi Polka"), Frankie Yankovic's "Who Stole the Kishka?" and Dave Stacy's "I Lost My Kielbasi."

The music grew increasingly important in setting the show's tone. Ron Sweed suggested material such as the instrumental rock album *The Ventures in Space*, which included the tune "The Bat." Two other songs have passed into legend.

One is a relatively obscure piece by Screamin' Jay Hawkins, a former Clevelander best known for "I Put a Spell on You," later covered by Creedence Clearwater Revival, a wild tune whose manic frenzy owes a lot to Hawkins and his band being drunk on Muscatel when they recorded it. "Constipation

QUEEN OF OUTER SPACE. A BOY, A GIRL, A RAY GUN.

SONGS IN THE KEY OF GHOULARDI

SONGS AND BITS OF SONGS, USUALLY UNIDENTIFIED ON THE AIR, PROVIDED BACKGROUND TO GHOULARDI MONOLOGUES, SKITS, AND FILMS. FANS STILL DEBATE WHAT THE SONGS WERE, WHETHER SONGS WERE HEARD WITH GHOULARDI OR THE GHOUL, AND WHICH VERSION OF A PARTICULAR SONG WAS PLAYED. THE FOLLOWING, AS FAR AS WE CAN DETERMINE, INCLUDES SONGS AND ARTISTS HEARD ON GHOULARDI'S SHOW. IT DOES NOT INCLUDE LATER GHOULARDI TRIBUTES BY BANDS LIKE THE CRAMPS AND THE EASTER MONKEYS (SEE CHAPTER 9).

"The Bat,"The Ventures

"The Bomb,"
Johnny & The Hurricanes

"Buzzsaw,"The Turtles

"Cherokee,"The Cherokees

"Constipation Blues,"
Screamin' Jay Hawkins

"Desert Rat," Duane Eddy

"Eddie's Blues," Eddie Cochran

"Ghoulardi Polka" ("Hej Gory Moje Gory"), John Borkowski Orchestra

"Greasy Spoon," Hank Marr

"Green Onions," Booker T & the MGs

"I Lost My Kielbasi,"
Dave Stacy Orchestra

"Incoherent Blues,"
The Oscar Peterson Trio

"I've Got a Woman," Jimmy McGriff

"Night Owl Blues,"
The Lovin' Spoonful

"Papa-Oom-Mow-Mow,"
The Rivingtons

"Peanuts (Lacacahuata),"
The Sunglows

"Pink Dominoes,"The Crescents

"Pygmy,"
Baby Stix and the Kingtones

"Rumble," Link Wray

"Silent Movies,"The Old Perfesser

"Space Rock, Parts One and Two,"
The Baskerville Hounds

"Stronger Than Dirt,"
Tom King and the Starfires

"Sugar Shack,"
Jimmy Gilmer & the Fireballs

"Surfin' Bird,"The Trashmen

"Turn Blue," Jimmy McGriff

Blues" was a song closer to his, uh, heart. It was inspired by Hawkins's own troubles with slow combustion.

"A subject like this must be put to music," he said. So he did, complete with grunts. Schodowski had heard about it from his friends at the foundry and introduced Ernie to it.

"He said, 'We've got to play it on the air,'" Schodowski recalled. "And I said, 'OK, but just play it up to the part where he's really grunting and it's obvious what he's doing.' So Ernie would purposely talk longer while the song was playing, so it would get into that [grunting] part." Management never caught on, Schodowski said, because "I would usually fade it out, so it never really got that bad. But Ernie would run right up to it sometimes."

The other unquestioned Ghoulardi classic is "Papa-Oom-Mow-Mow." Its driving beat and nonsensical chorus were in a rock and roll tradition that went back to the likes of the Silhouettes' "Get a Job" and continued with the Trashmen's "Surfin' Bird." Outside of Northeast Ohio, it was more likely to be heard in a cover version by the Beach Boys on their chart-topping 1964 *Beach Boys Concert* album. In Ghoulardi-land, the song is forever linked only to the Rivingtons—and the Gurning Man.

GHOULARDI AS
HE'S MOST OFTEN
REMEMBERED—
THE WIG, THE LAB
COAT, THE BUTTONS,
THE BEARD.

The dropped-in clips, gurning and otherwise, had to be laid out carefully for live TV. Schodowski and Soinski screened each movie in advance, and clocked the exact time in the movie to drop in the clips. "Like, four minutes and seventeen seconds into this segment, these guys get on a train," said Schodowski. It was a lot of work for mixed results. "A lot of times it worked, a lot of times it didn't."

But Ernie knew how important their contribution was. A 1963 *Cleveland Press* story noted: "Anderson feels that much of his success is due to the camera work of Chuck Schodowski and the film assistance of Bob Soinski." Ernie also told the national entertainment newspaper *Variety*, "I never imagined the show would catch on. Thanks, though, to Bob Soinski, the man who's furnished me with so many wonderful old film clips, and Chuck Schodowski, whose camera work for offbeat effects are [sic] so effective, we're clicking."

And clicking together. The collaborative nature of the relationship among Ernie, Schodowksi, and Soinski is exemplified by Ghoulardi's jumping into the films he hosted.

Ernie was not the first to use this technique. Elena Watson, in *Television Horror Movie Hosts*, traces it back to New York's John Zacherle. Schodowski, who put it in practice in Cleveland, was not aware of Zacherle's use of the technique. Rather, as a fan of television innovator Ernie Kovacs, Schodowski was eager to experiment with all the medium's possibilities.

In those years before Channel 8 had electronic character generators to project print on the screen, studio crews would put names in white letters against a black background on an easel, shoot the letters with one camera, and then superimpose them on the image from another camera or source.

Schodowski said: "I told Ernie, 'You know, if I can super [superimpose] this white name, then if you wear something white or light, I can put you in the movies.' That's where the white lab coat came from, and the white pants and white sneakers and white fright wig. We put a lot of white on him so he would key into the film . . . The white lab coat didn't start until we started putting him in the movies."

But what to do with Ghoulardi, once they found he could be dropped in to party with the undead, crab monsters, and giant behemoths? Schodowski figured that such a good gimmick deserved the same careful planning given the

"WHOAAA!"

dropped-in film clips from other movies.

"Bob Soinski and I would look at the films and mostly look for long scenes. In those cheap movies there are scenes that go three minutes without an edit [to another scene]." Things worked best when there was a long scene for Ernie to play with. He could suddenly appear next to a caveman eating his prey and offer to take him out for pizza. Or, Schodowski said, "This one movie in particular, I think it's *Dr. Cyclops*, there's a cave scene and a whole bunch of people running around, and he was there, and he was really good at it"— able to spontaneously react to, and joke about, the movie action around him, even though he was watching a confusing mirror image on a nearby monitor.

"I would look at the clock," Schodowski said, "and start telling him to get out" as the scene was ending.

But Ernie didn't always get out. "This one time he was really ad-libbing some funny stuff in *Attack of the 50-Foot Woman*. I think it was a cave again, and he was leaning against a wall. I look at the clock, and in about five seconds the scene is going to change, so I tell him, 'Get out, get out, get out.' And he's cracking a joke, and the cameramen are laughing and—boom!—the scene changes, and he has his right hand on the fifty-foot woman's boob. He looks at the monitor and goes, 'WHOAAA!'"

While the drop-ins were painstakingly worked out by Schodowski and Soinski, the improvisational quality of Ernie's comments was central to the show's appeal.

He did little preparation for the show. In fact, during the first *Shock Theater* telecast, Jack Riley recalled, "He was calling me for jokes . . . I was at home in Lakewood, and he was calling me for jokes."

Ernie worried that he rambled too much on the air, once saying that

ATTACK OF THE 50-FOOT WOMAN. LOOKING FOR A PLACE TO PLUG IN A 5-FOOT HAIR DRYER.

GHOULARDI
What Is This Thing Called Ghoulardi?

Ray Harrison calls himself
Mr. Boom-Boom.

He worked for more than twenty years in the fireworks industry, for companies in Ohio and Pennsylvania, traveling as far as the Orange Bowl to stage pyrotechnic displays that he says were "kind of like being in combat, to be honest with you. Load a mortar, boom, gone. Load a mortar, boom, gone."

He was just fourteen years old in 1963 when he started making the boom-booms for Ghoulardi. "Ernie probably used hundreds of my boom-booms over time," he said. "All of the heavy boom-booms were handmade by me and hand delivered.

"Pyrotechnics was something I was kind of fascinated in as a child. As a young kid I started getting all the books I could from the library, the Cleveland Public Library being one of the few libraries in the world that had an extensive pyrotechnic book collection. They'd bring me books written as far back as the 1700s and 1800s."

Harrison claims he was just thirteen when he was offered a job at a commercial fireworks factory, "after demonstrating some of the items I had been working on." The fireworks for Ghoulardi were the result of experiments in his family's basement, and "a few were experiments that weren't supposed to do what they did," he said. "But nobody ever got hurt down there. That was the most important thing."

He worked with a friend, Joe Sprosty, "who was good with his hands ... He would make things like dummies of Dorothy Fuldheim and model cars to blow up." On

Friday nights, Harrison would walk three miles to Southland Shopping Center from his home in Middleburg Heights, catch a bus to Public Square in downtown Cleveland, and then walk fifteen blocks to WJW.

He and Sprosty would follow the alley to the back door, ring a buzzer, talk to someone on the intercom—"I never did know who I was talking to"—and drop off their goods for Ernie. "He was a real kind of open-minded guy," Harrison said. "Spontaneous. He lit those fuses.

"Everything we dropped off he used. After about three weeks, he left word with the guard he wanted to meet us. He said, 'Man, I like the stuff you guys are bringing down.' He had us maybe a half dozen times on the air, and had us explain what we do. Then we got to hang around and watch the show.

"I started bringing the heavy stuff down—to the point where Don Quigley would leave the camera and the studio when the fuse was lit. Everyone cleared out of the studio, including myself. They were getting a little outrageous for indoor use. Big Chuck was concerned about the place burning down or actually blowing up. I think he thought I was kind of a Unabomber kind of guy.

"I remember Ernie got a letter from the fire marshal telling him not to shoot any more fireworks. He put it on the stand with one of my boom-booms and blew it up. He had confidence in my stuff. He knew people

wouldn't get killed."

"Some of the real loud stuff was a mistake," Harrison admitted. But he was careful never to use any kind of metal ("or else you get shrapnel") and never had any duds because he used "fail-safe" materials. His advice for handling a dud is unequivocal: "Don't go near it."

Harrison's parents permitted him to make the late-night trek to WJW because they felt he would be safe. "Things weren't as crazy as they are nowadays," he said. His father, who was blind, worked as a musician and would commonly arrive home via public transportation in the middle of the night. As for the fireworks, "my mother was tolerant of it, even though I caused a ruckus in the neighborhood. I never went to jail over it."

Harrison, who got his first paying job in fireworks at eighteen, left the field in the early 1990s to work with his wife in eldercare. "I'm still in one piece, I've got all my fingers and toes.

"When you're shooting fireworks, you're an entertainer, but nobody sees you," he said. "I kind of regretted in some ways going in the direction I did with the fireworks career," he said. "I could have done better going into theatrical rather than display pyrotechnics, meaning the movies. That's big money."

having a movie saved him from having to talk too much. "Ernie had to be entertaining all the time," said Schodowski, and inspiration could come from anywhere.

Including a cornfield. During a drive to the studio with Ron Sweed, Ernie once spotted a field full of fresh corn. He stopped his car to heist an armload, and cooked it on the cob in a studio kitchenette as part of that night's telecast.

Sweed, who later starred in his own movie host role as the Ghoul, marvelled at Ernie's easy inspiration. "I'd start on Monday and work until Thursday, trying to format twelve good bits. I just don't have the talent that Ernie has, or else I could do a whole night's show on corn."

Soinski said that as Ghoulardi, Ernie "got to do the thing he wanted to do, rather than just be a straight man." And Ernie was making as much mischief as he could—not likely to let any of the suits in management in on his plans. "Don't you get in trouble with Ernie," Schodowski recalls being warned by one friendly station manager.

On a live show, there was no tape to edit in advance, no way to stop him from perpetrating some midnight madness. As Ghoulardi became a sensation, management could not risk killing the show, but they kept trying to rein it in. "Every Monday, Ernie was up on the carpet—'You'd better not do this again,'" said Schodowski.

Soinski once asked Ernie if he ever sought permission for his wilder stunts. Ernie's reply: "Oh, no. I don't ask for permission because if I did, they'd tell me don't do it. If I wasn't sure about it, they certainly wouldn't allow me to do it. If I ever did anything they didn't appreciate, they'd tell me 'Don't do it again,' but meanwhile I've had it on the air.'"

How wild could Ghoulardi get? How about attacking the grande dame of local broadcasting, a couple of beloved children's-show icons, and a hot star of Cleveland TV who was becoming a national name?

Ernie chose the targets of his barbs by some internal process blending a distaste for the revered and powerful with sheer caprice. Ernie often said that all he asked of people was that they be honest. "If I picked on somebody, I picked on them for a damn good reason," he told *Ohio Magazine* in 1978. Ghoulardi's attacks did not always have to do with a specific objection to the target, however; it just seemed fun to mock Cleveland's sacred.

Few in Cleveland media were held in higher esteem than Dorothy Fuldheim. Born in 1893, she was an accomplished lecturer when Ernie was still in short pants and had been doing commentary and interviews on WEWS for more than fifteen years before Ghoulardi uttered his first "Cool it."

GHOULARDI MOVIES

UNREAL ESTATE

Terror in the Haunted House (1958).

The Unseen (1945).
Eerie vacant house.

Island of Lost Souls (1932).

THAT VOODOO YOU DO SO WELL

The Disembodied (1957).

The Invisible Menace (1938).

DAYS OF FUTURE AND PAST

World Without End (1956).
Astronauts battle creatures on 26th-century Earth.

One Million B.C. (1940).
Prehistoric epic.

KARLOFFUL PERFORMANCES

Horror-movie star Boris Karloff was often seen on *Ghoulardi* as host and sometime star of *Thriller*, the 1960–62 TV anthology, episodes of which were shown in place of movies. Karloff films were also on view, from his classic monster turn in *Frankenstein* (1932) to the amnesiac writer in *The Haunted Strangler* (1958).

THE BAT.
OOOOOHHHH, SCARY!

"That was the last person you'd say anything bad about," Schodowski said.

But Fuldheim's on-air performances also revealed a certain rhetorical windiness and metaphorical incoherence that Ernie could have chewed on like the fancy steaks he loved. (He once snatched a steak away from a guest about to put A-1 sauce on it.) Instead of attacking her where she might take offense, however, he ridiculed her appearance—which, despite her flashy wardrobe and famously flaming red hair, was a far cry from glamorous. Fuldheim herself claimed no concern about her looks; as an example of her lack of vanity, she once told about having to borrow a comb from a cabbie because she did not carry one.

Ernie dropped her photo into movie scenes where characters were recoiling in horror from an image or studying the photograph of some strange beast. He had her picture displayed on the set, and his wild exclamation of "DOOR-othy!" became a catchword that was endlessly repeated by fans.

According to Ernie, at least, he and Fuldheim had no problems and even made occasional personal appearances together. "She understood exactly what I was doing," he said, in a 1993 *Beacon Journal* interview.

But Schodowski says Ernie was ultimately told to stop making fun of her.

Making fun of the kids-show hosts was another example of Ghoulardi logic.

Captain Penny, played by Ron Penfound, was an amiable soul in a trainman's cap and overalls hosting Three Stooges shorts and Little Rascals comedies on WEWS; Linn Sheldon's Barnaby, a pointy-eared leprechaun with a string tie and straw hat, held court with Popeye cartoons on KYW. To the kids drawn to Ghoulardi, a youthful audience lurching toward adolescence and *Famous Monsters of Filmland,* these warm-hearted hosts were small-fry fare—the video equivalent of *Highlights for Children.* (Their delight in Ghoulardi's jibes was paralleled in the playground backlash of later years against Barney, the sickly-sweet purple dinosaur, in which kids tried to demonstrate their sophistication by turning Barney's affectionate "I love you, you love me" ditty into a snarled "I hate you, you hate me . . .")

CAPTAIN PENNY (RONALD PENFOUND) WITH FANS.

DOOR-othy!'

If Ernie needed more reason to mock them than that his audience would enjoy it, he could have found it in Captain Penny's endless, and some would say preachy, reminders to kids not to imitate the Three Stooges. Ernie reminded his own fans that Captain Penny was "someone I wouldn't give a nickel for."

Sheldon, at least, later said that he took no offense from Ghoulardi's barbs at Barnaby. In a way, it was flattering to be satirized.

Mike Douglas might not have felt flattered. Emerging as a major star from his daytime talk show on KYW, he was not only a Ghoulardi target but a figure with whom Ernie had a complicated, and probably one-sided, emotional relationship.

Ghoulardi literally turned Douglas into a cardboard Saint Stephen, firing darts at a life-size cutout of the talk-show host. WJW news photographer Ralph Tarsitano said the bit started in the station basement, where Ernie worked out of a cubbyhole next to the photographers' ready room. A dartboard hung on the wall, not far from where Ernie had capriciously displayed a glossy publicity photo of Douglas. It became standard practice for photographers to lob darts past the board and into Douglas's mugshot. The bit soon moved upstairs and onto TV.

MIKE DOUGLAS, LEFT, AND LINN "BARNABY" SHELDON, RIGHT, WITH MCDONALDS RESTAURANTS' REPRESENTATIVE BERNARD STREETER. SHELDON WAS A TOP COMMERCIAL SPOKESMAN FOR THE BURGER CHAIN.

The Mike Douglas Show, where the host said his job was always to make the guest look good, ran counter to Ernie's on-air philosophy. At the same time, though, Douglas—whose show was bound for national syndication in August 1963—seemed to stand in the way of Ernie's dream of conquering Cleveland and moving beyond it.

Douglas's life followed a path similar to Ernie's. Like Ernie, he had come far from undistinguished beginnings—in Douglas's case, on the West Side of Chicago, where he was born in 1925. As a singer and broadcast personality, he had been something of a gypsy; Cleveland, which he liked and made his summer home in the '90s, was not his last career stop any more than it was Ernie's. Mild-mannered on the air, Douglas could get steely-eyed off camera. He liked being the top man in his field, and expected respect for his accomplishments.

Moreover, neither man was an overnight sensation. Douglas was 36 when he made it in Cleveland, Ernie 39 when he began playing Ghoulardi.

But there the similarities end. The two approached TV differently, one asking the audience to like him, the other daring viewers to hate his bewhiskered persona. Ernie married three times; Douglas's marriage has lasted more than fifty years. Douglas inspired Rosie O'Donnell. Ernie inspired the Ghoul.

While Douglas should have been just another target for Ghoulardi— Schodowski summed up their rivalry as "just a professional ego thing"— Ernie nursed his resentment toward Douglas long after both had ankled

Cleveland for new fortune and fame. In the '80s, Ernie said Douglas had not spoken to him since the Ghoulardi years. He declared variously that Douglas "had no sense of humor" and was "a dullard."

Ernie also claimed that when he and Conway had gone on the road in the late '60s to promote one of their comedy albums, he was turned away from Douglas's show, which could have provided enormous national exposure for the act. "He said, 'Tim Conway can come on, but Ernie Anderson can't,'" Ernie said.

As is so often the case with Ernie's stories, other people's recollections differ. Douglas flatly denies banning Ernie from his show, claiming that his producer, Woody Fraser, was too close to Ernie for that to have happened. "So was Tim Conway. We had Tim on, and Tim and Ernie Anderson were inseparable buddies."

Contending that he did not get involved in booking guests on the show, Douglas called the banning story "absolute garbage. Now that the man is no longer with us, I wish I had known that [story] sooner so I could have told him."

As for how he felt about Ghoulardi's jibes, Douglas said, "I don't want to sound naive, but I couldn't watch that show because I was working all the time. I really don't know what he was doing on the air."

Conway did remember some kind of Douglas ban, although he had to be asked specifically about it, and still was not sure the reason was what Ernie imagined. "I guess [Douglas] figured, 'Conway is the one doing the comedy on the thing,'" Conway said. "He probably considered Ernie a straight man." In other words, Douglas saw Ernie in the same terms Steve Allen had when he invited Conway but not Ernie out West. Still, Conway said of the Douglas situation, "Ernie was kind of upset about it."

Fraser wondered if Ernie's antagonism toward Douglas dated from an earlier snub. "I know that in the beginning [of the Douglas show], we had talked about having an announcer," said Fraser. "We auditioned about six people, and Ernie was by far the best. But I just didn't have it in the budget, when it came down to it . . . Maybe Ernie was upset that he didn't get the announcing job."

Whatever his reasons for attacking Douglas and other local stars (including Bill "Smoochie" Gordon of WEWS, a pal who visited the set—but became "Bill Gorgon" to Ghoulardi), at least those attacks dealt with subjects familiar to Ernie's audience. Sometimes, his jokes were deliberately obscure, as if Ernie were a standup comic playing to the band—or as if he cared only about amusing himself.

Most of the approximately twenty skits filmed for the show had a universal appeal, especially when Ernie played a poor soul pantomiming troubles on a date or at a bowling alley. An Ajax detergent commercial of the time portrayed a white knight riding through residential neighborhoods, waving his lance and cleansing laundry hanging on clotheslines. "Stronger than dirt," the ad proclaimed, inspiring both a song of the same name (by the Cleveland band Tom King and the Starfires, which later evolved into the Outsiders, of "Time Won't Let Me" fame) and an accompanying bit for Ghoulardi.

"Ernie did a skit (to the song) where he was riding on his horse late one night," Schodowski said. "The funny thing was that the horse would panic when you'd approach him with that big lance. As long as you didn't have the lance you could get on the horse, but as soon as he saw the lance he'd go crazy. We had to shoot the scene where Ernie would run by, like he was on the horse." The surviving tape is even funnier because of the cuts between the knight on horseback, without the lance, and the knight with the lance, obviously running.

But two skits in particular seemed designed not for the mass audience but for a small band of viewers whom Ernie imagined sharing his bent sensibilities.

The most notorious was nothing but *Gunsmoke* and mirrors. Titled "The Stranger," it was an elaborate filmed parody of *Gunsmoke,* the long-running Western series on which Ernie had a three-line part in 1964. Originally a half-hour weekly drama, the show expanded to an hour in 1961. Ernie came back from his appearance claiming, "They've got these half-hour scripts and they've just made every scene twice as long . . . You'd just say twice as many things." With no patience for long waits on TV and movie soundstages, Ernie was exasperated by the notion and decided to demonstrate *Gunsmoke*'s folly in a painfully drawn-out skit.

"He was Marshal Dillon," said Schodowski, "and I was the Stranger, and every piece of dialogue was twice as long as it should have been." Schodowski and Soinski, who also played the marshal's sidekick Quigley, had tried to rescue the skit by coming up with some jokes between the time of Ernie's brainstorm and the actual filming. Still, Schodowski said, Ernie refused to explain to the audience the point of the skit, which ended up just dull.

"It was about eighteen minutes long and it was really boring,"

said Schodowski, exaggerating neither the length nor the tedium. "He had a scene where he said, 'Let me think,' and he thought for about a minute, just to kill time."

VIDEO ADVENTURES

Like the TV series *Thriller* before it, *The Outer Limits,* a fantasy anthology which ran on ABC from 1963 to 1965, was rerun as part of *Ghoulardi.* In the early 1980s Stephen King called *The Outer Limits* "the best program of its type ever to run on network TV." A new version appeared in the mid-1990s.

VARIOUS WEIRDNESS

Spy in the Sky (1958). U.S. and Russia search for German space expert.

The Hypnotic Eye (1960). Women mutilate themselves after participating in hypnotism.

Ghost Diver (1957). Search for undersea treasure.

Saadia (1953). Romantic triangle with dancing girl.

The Moonraker (1958). Not the James Bond flick but an English costume drama.

Valley of the Kings (1954). Pyramids, thieves, swordplay, Biblical theory.

White Witch Doctor (1953). Lavish jungle tale.

Some of the skit had been filmed in a bar, with real customers out of camera range, laughing at the performers' flubs. "When I was editing the film," Soinski said, "I saw these outtakes, the goofups and all the laughter. I said we ought to put together a show of the outtakes, but Ernie wouldn't do it. He just wanted to do the *Gunsmoke* skit." In the face of repeated entreaties to explain the skit, Ernie insisted, "The hip people are going to see."

Ernie more aggressively tested the tolerance of his viewers and his bosses' tolerance with a filmed piece Soinski calls "The Bomb."

"After the show, Chuck and Ernie and I would go to this bar a couple of doors away," he said. "We called it the Swamp, but it was the Seagram's Bar. Terrific cheeseburgers, and Ernie would always buy us a stein of Michelob. You could never buy for him. That was one of his ways of paying us back. So we'd go there and have a couple beers and talk over the show and think up ideas for future skits.

"Well, one time, because the Cold War was a big thing, Ernie came up with the idea to do a skit about the Cold War and the bomb. He usually played the 'poor soul' character in these skits, and in this one he was coming home from work in Parma. And up in the righthand corner was a countdown clock, counting down whatever the length of the skit was. Eight minutes or whatever." As Ernie went about his business, he turned on the TV, "and there he sees shots of the United Nations. I used some news film, shots of Kennedy, Khrushchev, De Gaulle. And I used shots of Ernie doing things, then back to the United Nations. And as the count got closer to zero, the shots were quicker and quicker. And when it got down to a few seconds, we got down to one-frame edits so it's just flying around, and you got the sense that something was happening. And when it got to zero, you saw this big mushroom cloud, the bomb. And then right after that, we went to hash [a snowy screen], like we actually got bombed and went off the air for a long time, at least thirty seconds, which was a long time on the air."

"It was not a funny skit," said Soinski, "but it was a message that Ernie wanted to portray."

Viewers complained. On Monday, Soinski said, "the operational supervisor came to me and said, '"The Bomb" bombed. Don't ever do that again.' But Ernie liked it, he was happy, and that was all that mattered as far as he was concerned."

"That's really a statement," said Tarsitano, who shot the street scenes and clock for the film. "That was his mind. That was a heck of a piece."

Just as mass-appeal gags like the Mike Douglas jokes went hand in hand with Ernie's more self-absorbed "Bomb" and *Gunsmoke* skits, so did those supposedly hip pieces coexist with the unambiguously anarchic mayhem that firecrackers would visit upon objects on camera.

GHOULARDI

Chapter 3

The Lost Man

WHILE GHOULARDI WAS A PHENOMENAL SUCCESS FOR ERNIE, CHANNEL 8, AND MOST OF THE PEOPLE INVOLVED IN THE SHOW, RALPH GULKO DID NOT SHARE IN THE SUCCESS. THE MAN WHO HAD GIVEN THE CHARACTER A FACE AND A NAME SAID, "I GOT RIPPED OFF GOOD."

"I didn't know about registering something," he said. "I got paid for a few things. I had a chance and I hit it. I didn't give the station anything in writing. I thought they were going to take care of me, and they didn't."

At first, Gulko said, he was told there was a shortage of funds to compensate him. But as Ghoulardi turned into a windfall for WJW, none of it hit Gulko.

"They bounced me around," he said. "Why, I'll never know. I was going to get a lawyer, but I was talked out of it by Howard Hoffmann."

"I told him at the time that he was fighting a brick wall," said Hoffmann, who had his own scraps with station management over the years. "You're like fighting city hall with that outfit."

Neither Gulko nor Hoffmann blamed Ernie or harbored any resentment toward him.

"Ernie was a special type of guy. Sometimes," Hoffman said with a chuckle, "he'd take advantage for his own prosperity. I worked his shift for three days while he went off to Ohio Bell [on a commercial job] and made nineteen hundred bucks." During Hoffmann's weather reports, Ernie sometimes would stand off-camera, trying to crack him up. "He'd open his fly and pull out his shirt, he'd do anything for a laugh."

"Ernie got into the character," Gulko said. "He was a terrific performer and he made it different every time. I loved to see it on TV and know I had something to do with it. It was a dream come true. I just didn't get credit for it is all, and I was heartbroken."

However vividly Ernie fleshed out Gulko's vision, Gulko's bitterness over not being recognized for his contribution was far greater than any financial disappointment he might have felt. He left Cleveland late in 1964 for Los Angeles, where he became a makeup artist—first at ABC and then, starting in 1968, at NBC, where he spent eleven years on Johnny Carson's *Tonight* show.

Those years and the ones that followed were a mixture of joy and disappointment for Gulko. In his sunset years, he still longed for some formal acknowledgment of his role in Ghoulardi's history.

Asked what that kind of recognition would mean, Gulko, his eyes misting, said, "I would love it. Everybody dreams of something that stands out. I would love to show that to my family."

"I don't think anybody thought of ripping Ralph off," said Shelley Saltman, promotion manager at WJW in 1963. "But somebody should recognize that Ralph Gulko initiated this idea. I don't know if there's any monetary value in it—probably nothing. But the point is, I think he's always felt, and rightly so, that nobody said, 'Hey—he came up with the idea.'"

RALPH GULKO, CREATOR OF THE GHOULARDI CHARACTER (SITTING) WITH SHELDON SALTMAN.

GHOULARDI PREPARES TO BLOW UP A GIFT FROM A FAN.

Literally blowing things up seemed a natural extension of Ghoulardi's verbal fireworks. When firecrackers arrived at WJW, by mail or hand-delivered by fans, Ernie brought them into the studio, set them on a small table beside him, and blew them up—usually lighting the fuse with a cigarette or cigar.

Sometimes he blew up only the fireworks. More often, as time went on, he would use them to blow up plastic models sent in by fans. Occasionally, he could take unnecessary risks with himself and the people around him. Ron Sweed, who assembled the show's array of pyrotechnics, said he became the "official firework lighter" when Ernie was unsure what would happen if he lit a particular item.

Sweed recalled one Saturday when he and Ernie's oldest son, Mike, were helping around the set. Ernie was down at Pierre's, and Mike and Ron were assembling the set for the Saturday show. "Ernie knew right where his beard and mustache would be, by his lab coat, by his fright wig. And right by his beard and mustache on the table I'd always have a big box of firecrackers, so he could just light them at will while he was talking," Sweed said.

"Mike and I had set everything up, and we were all done. We had boxes of models and stuff to blow up, tons of stuff that Ernie would never get to. So some nights, just to amuse ourselves, we'd light off models. There was this big, long cylindrical rocket, and I said, 'Mike, why don't you light the rocket?' 'That's a big one. Naw, you light the rocket.' So I set it on the round stand that we did all our blow-ups on, and I lit the fuse, and this thing was not an indoor firework.

"It just took off and was doing circles around the studio. And it wouldn't stop, it just kept going, shooting sparks everywhere. It started the curtain on fire—the big, $5,000 cyclorama backdrop that we used. It has great big holes in it, and it's smoking and everything. Then the sparks flew into the box of firecrackers, and—wham! bam! bang! bam!—the whole box went off.

"By this time, the Hungarian engineer has come by. Mike is just standing there with his mouth wide open, just in shock, as I am. This engineer, who did not like Ernie Anderson, who did not like Big Chuck or Hoolihan either, came by—and we're relieved to have a responsible adult there—and said, 'That's really good! Just burn down the whole [bleep] studio! See if I care!'"

The rocket stopped, the boys found a fire extinguisher, and the smoke cleared. But Ernie's beard and mustache had been incinerated—and it was just five minutes to showtime. Sweed nervously brought the news to Pierre's; Ernie laughed and sent him to a desk drawer for a spare beard and mustache.

"Cool it with the boom-booms."

Ernie wasn't laughing later, though, when he saw the curtain had burned, too. He showed the damage to viewers as a reminder of why he said, "Cool it with the boom-booms."

The fun with explosives ended, Ernie ruefully admitted, "when I almost blew up the building."

"This one thing was sent in," Schodowski recalled, "and I told Ernie, 'You'd better not light this one.' It was much too heavy to be a firecracker, it was like a military thing, sort of khaki. I said it could be a plastic explosive or something, it's just too dense." But Schodowski had made a mistake in telling Ernie not to light the piece, because Ernie inevitably took such warnings as a challenge. He took the bomb with him on the air.

"He put on this big helmet and he put on these safety glasses, and I said, yep, he's going to light it," Schodowski said. "He took a big drag on his cigar and lit it and sort of eased out of the shot."

The explosion shook the studio, its force driving the glass in the control room so far inward that Schodowski was amazed it did not break. Soinski was in the projection room, which was another wall farther back from the studio behind the control room, and still felt a blast of sound so strong, "My ears just blocked."

"There was nothing in the studio but smoke and flames, and the drapes were all on fire," Schodowski said. "We went to commercial, and went and got every fire extinguisher in the station, because we didn't want to call the fire department. Everybody was just putting out fires, and fires, and fires. We opened up the doors to let all the smoke out, but the next couple of breaks it was still smoky."

The incident was not mentioned on the air. Still, the fire department came to the station on Monday, to be greeted by a lobby full of two dozen emptied fire extinguishers. The word came down: Ernie had to permanently cool it with the boom-booms.

Such incidents might suggest that being around Ernie was dangerous

WARMING UP IN THE STUDIO.

GHOULARDI MOVIES

THEY CAME FROM THE BOWERY

Bowery Boy comedies from 1946–58 were shown on *Ghoulardi* many Saturdays beginning in 1964. Among them: *Blonde Dynamite, Blues Busters, Bowery Buckaroos, Bowery Boys Meet the Monsters, Feudin' Fools, Hard Boiled Mahoney, Hold That Baby!, Hold That Hypnotist, In Fast Company, Paris Playboys,* and *Smugglers' Cove.*

CAPERS IN COLOR

The first film shown in color on *Ghoulardi*, after Channel 8 began color telecasts in March 1964, was *House of Wax* on March 5. Some color movies, such as *Dr. Cyclops* and *Queen of Outer Space*, were originally shown in black-and-white on *Ghoulardi*, then rerun in color.

THE BOWERY BOYS, A SATURDAY STAPLE BEGUN IN 1964, STAR IN HARDBOILED MAHONEY.

business, and that anyone willing to spend much time with him was at risk. But co-workers remember mostly fun.

"If you weren't doing anything Friday night, and you were off, you went to the station," Ralph Tarsitano said. "Ernie's . . . playing football on the set, throwing baseballs. He was part of making Channel 8 a family."

The after-show bull and drinking sessions are fondly remembered, and Ernie loved them.

Soinski, who was more determined than Schodowski to stay out of Ernie's off-camera adventures, still has a reservoir of affectionate stories. When Soinski's son was born in 1961, while Tim Conway and Ernie were doing *Ernie's Place*, "They did a whole routine about receiving a gift from me," he said. "They brought on this huge tubular thing and did a whole routine about what it was. At the end of the show they unwrapped it, and it was a big cigar. I thought these were pretty good guys."

When Soinski and Ernie were both working the late shift, Ernie had to do a brief newscast after the second late movie ended. It didn't start until about 1:00 a.m., and Ernie would ask Soinski to time exactly when it was going to end, to see if they could make it to a local bar before closing time at 3:30. "He'd say, 'Have everything on the projectors for the morning, and be ready to run out the door as soon as the national anthem is over.' We did that four or five times—hop on Ernie's motorcycle, run there, put down a couple quick steins of beer or couple of shots, and get back on the motorcycle."

Pals would stop by during the show, including Jack Riley, Tim Conway, Bill Gordon, and Jay Lawrence from KYW radio. Soinski recalled a private performance by Conway, whom he knew from KYW. The station switchboard was closed at night, and phone calls were sometimes routed to the projection room, where Conway hung out. "He'd answer the phone and have fun with people. One time he was pretending like he was an answering machine. He'd say, 'When you hear the tone, leave your name,' and they'd say, 'My name is so-and-so,' and he'd beep and say, 'No, you didn't say it fast enough. You have to get your message in between the tones. Now try it again.' And he beeps, and then beeps again, and they're talking real fast."

"Another time," Soinski said, "he had a list of programming for the whole week. He had somebody on the phone and said, 'Ernie can't come to the phone right now, but while you're waiting, don't forget to watch Channel 8. On Monday at 6:00 a. m., it's sign-on; 6:30 a. m., Sunrise Semester.' And he keeps going, reading until they hang up."

But being part of Ernie's inner circle was demanding. He partied hard and liked his friends to party with him. He also enjoyed practical jokes that, until the punchline was clear, did not have the object laughing. Both Soinski and Schodowski were victims of one such trick.

"He had his motorcycle," Schodowski recalled, "and said, 'Come on, I'll take you around the block.' So we went down to the Shoreway, going like 90, 100 miles an hour." A commercial break was coming up before they left, and they were supposed to be at the station, Ernie to lead into the break and Schodowski to do the technical work.

As they rode along, time ticking by, "I figure we're going to get to the point of no return, where I'm not going to get back in time," Schodowski said. "And that point is reached, and I figure I'm fired." Ernie drove all the way home to Willoughby, a silent Schodowski with him. They had a beer, Ernie had a bite to eat, and finally they went back to the station—where Schodowski discovered that another engineer had helped Ernie prerecord his breaks and had done Schodowski's work. All just so Ernie could scare him.

Ernie also expected Schodowski and Soinski to become part of his repertory company, performing in televised skits. Neither did so easily, and while Soinski appeared in a few pieces, including the *Gunsmoke* skit, he generally ducked Ernie's determination to make him a star.

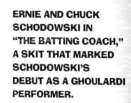

Schodowski was another matter. He helped Ernie, drank with him, wrote jokes for him. Still, when Ernie wanted him to go on camera, "I said, 'No way.' I was basically quiet and shy. Always have been. And I was terrified.

"One day, he said, 'What size pants do you wear?' I said, 'What are you doing?' He said, 'Never mind. What do you take, a 42 jersey?' I said, 'What are you doing?' He said, 'Nothing. I'm getting you an Indians uniform, and you're going to play a batting coach.'

"I said, 'No, I can't do it,'" Schodowski said. "He said, 'Trust me.'"

Schodowski worried for days, especially because Ernie ad-libbed his comments most of the time, "and I couldn't do that." When the time came to do the skit, he was still resisting. "Ernie got three of the biggest guys around, and they literally pantsed me in the studio. I knew then that it would be easier to do the skit than go through all of this."

The bit was a simple build-up to a punchline: The coach used to work for the Mets, then the worst team in baseball, and Schodowski proved unable even to hit a ball tossed lightly in the air. "The only reason I liked it was that Ernie put me in as a character that I really was," Schodowski said. "I was scared, like someone who was not on TV might be. And I looked like an

ERNIE AND CHUCK SCHODOWSKI IN "THE BATTING COACH," A SKIT THAT MARKED SCHODOWSKI'S DEBUT AS A GHOULARDI PERFORMER.

GHOULARDI
What Is This Thing Called Ghoulardi?

athlete, so it looked believable. It was so believable, some people really thought it was real, and that was Ernie's kind of humor."

But Ernie wasn't done with Schodowski. He had a special coming up, Conway was returning to town for it, and Ernie again wanted Schodowski, this time as a singer. Again, Schodowski didn't want to be in it.

"I had a week [of vacation] coming. So I took the week Ernie was going to tape the special, and we went to Kelleys Island. I didn't tell a soul where I was going. Nobody knew. About the third day, we were at Kelleys Island, and a cop came up and said, 'There's a call for you from Ernie Anderson.'" Schodowski, who never learned how Ernie had found him, knew he was licked and went back to do the special, performing in a strange bit that plays as a very inside joke: Ernie gave Schodowski an enormous build-up, then put him on a wobbly set to sing off-key. There was no explanation that Schodowski was deliberately off-key, he simply did it. Like the *Gunsmoke* bit, Ernie figured the hip people would get it.

Schodowski began appearing with more frequency in televised skits, especially in the notorious "Parma Place." He eventually became comfortable enough to perform without Ernie on the Ghoulardi show's successors, *Hoolihan & Big Chuck* and *Big Chuck and Lil' John*. He still credits Ernie. "He saw something in me that I didn't see."

Always, they looked for new material. After the premiere of *Laurel, Ghoulardi and Hardy*, a weekday show for kids, Soinski suggested a show about painting the set. Then he came up with a visual gag: painting the set with stripes.

"We didn't have the electronic gadgets then," Soinski said, "so Ernie said, 'How can we do that?' And it just came to my mind to divide the can of paint with a divider, put two different colors of paint in there, and cut off a few bristles in the middle of the brush." That effectively created two brushes on a single handle, and each brush could dip into one of the separate sides of the paint can. "And it worked," Soinski said. "This led to somebody else thinking of cutting holes in a paint roller and making polka-dot paint."

Schodowski thinks the Beatles were seen for the first time on Cleveland television on the Ghoulardi show. Seen, but not heard.

"CBS would send down news feeds," he said. "They sent down this tape of these guys, I couldn't even remember their names. They were from England and they had these weird haircuts. I told Ernie, 'You've got to see this group. They're really big in England.' He looks at 'em: 'They look so funny.' Ernie was going to show them on the air, and I said, take the lead-in to it, the CBS announcer saying 'the hottest group in England is about to come to America, and we'll give you a little sampling of one of their songs.' And what I did was cut out [the song] and play 'Who Stole the Kishka?' And it was real funny because it was almost in tempo."

The fun could have a cruel edge, however. Even close friend Schodowski thought Ernie had crossed the line of fair play in one studio bit inspired by Ernie's visit to a dog-training class.

"He was telling me about it and crying, he was laughing so hard," Schodowski said. "'You won't believe this,' he said. 'The dogs aren't trained, the people are. They play the music and the people do these steps exactly.' So he had them down on the show, and there were some old people in the group, and I thought, 'We're gonna get killed.'

"He was right, the people had the steps down perfect but they were dragging the dogs. Two dogs are fighting, and one dog is kind of taking a crap, and we've got shots of this on the air. And Ernie is in the middle of it, pretending they're really doing something."

As Schodowski had feared, "We got blasted." One of the newspapers went after Ernie for the stunt. "The station was inundated with 'how cruel,' 'how terrible,' 'it's the lowest thing he's ever done.' Ernie was really on the carpet, but he said, 'Aw, people can't take a joke,'" said Schodowski. He told Ernie the display was sad, but Ernie was unrepentant.

A few weeks later, after the fuss had died down, Ernie invited the dog-training class back on the show. They came. Ernie said, "There they are. Don't blame me."

Naturally, the resulting performance duplicated the first.

"Ernie was a visionary," said Shelley Saltman, the WJW promotions chief who helped create Ghoulardi and then left for a successful career as a promoter in Hollywood. "Nobody does it by himself, but he saw something no one else saw, and he made it happen. It was his persona, his personality, that made it happen."

GHOULARDI MOVIES

CRIME TIME

Plunder Road (1958). Thieves steal gold from train.

Please Murder Me (1956). Attorney, in love with murderous client, asks her to kill him.

The Gracie Allen Murder Case (1939). The dizzy half of Burns and Allen hooks up with detective Philo Vance.

The Abductors (1957). Kidnapping, body snatching.

Murder with Pictures (1936). Hit man works as newspaper photographer.

She Asked for It (1937). Husband-wife team investigate murder.

Street of Chance (1942). Amnesiac implicated in murder.

Stop, You're Killing Me (1952). Ex-bootlegger tries to go straight.

The Strip (1951). Drummer gets involved with crooks.

"Aw, people can't take a joke."

GHOULARDI
What Is This Thing
Called Ghoulardi?

CHAPTER 4

The Best Location

A lot of people would remember the summer of 1963 as the real end of the 1950s. It was the giddy final season before the Kennedy assassination and the turbulent "long, hot summers" of the 1960s . . .

GHOULARDI MUGS IN A 1963 INDIANS UNIFORM.

It was a time when adolescence was evolving into a cult but not yet a culture; a summer of "Fun, Fun, Fun" and "Surf City," "Heat Wave" and "Fingertips," cherry Impalas and fire-engine Galaxies.

If Cleveland was giddy, that giddiness was earned. Clevelanders talk about earning their sunshine with snowstorms, and buying their breaks with adversity. That year both snow and adversity had seemed all too common.

In January 1963, Cleveland was a place ready for something good to happen.

Winter had arrived with a crippling snowstorm before Halloween and hardened into the worst deep-freeze in 100 years, piling up record snowfalls by December and plunging the mercury to a record twenty degrees below zero a month later.

Paul Brown, the legendary coach of the Cleveland Browns, had just been fired by the team's relatively new owner, Art Modell, in a move that stunned the city and outraged fans who already were reeling from an earlier bombshell: the news that Ernie Davis, the Heisman Trophy–winning halfback from Syracuse who was supposed to join Jim Brown in Cleveland's 1963 backfield, had leukemia.

The suddenly hapless Cleveland Indians, still smarting from the trade of Rocky Colavito, were coming off a sixth-place season in the American League—the third of what would become nine second-division finishes in the decade. General manager Gabe Paul had also unveiled their new uniforms for 1963: ugly, sleeveless, vest-style jerseys over shirts that resembled long underwear. Given the state of Tribe pitching, wags suggested that the vests be bulletproof.

The downtown Inner Belt Freeway, just completed in 1962, was disclosing a serious design flaw where it met the Shoreway—a tendency to make cars and trucks flip over, spin out, or jackknife at a hairpin that became known, all but officially, as Dead Man's Curve.

Anthony J. Celebrezze, a mayor so popular he won an unprecedented five terms, had been tapped for a cabinet job in Washington as secretary of housing and urban development. While the Erieview Redevelopment Project, ultimately encompassing office towers and a glittering mall, would become his greatest legacy, in 1963 the short-term legacies were his successor, the colorless caretaker Ralph Locher, and a downtown dotted with bulldozed lots.

Downtown Cleveland was in the middle of a building boom, but the determined air of civic optimism was as self-conscious as could be expected in a city that many felt was still convalescing from the Depression.

Despite the claim of being "The Best Location in the Nation," first advanced in advertising for The Illuminating Company in 1944, Cleveland was ambivalent about itself—always a city "in search of an image," as longtime *Plain Dealer* columnist George Condon noted in his 1967 book, *Cleveland: The Best Kept Secret*.

"It can be taken as an absolute axiom," he wrote, "that . . .

there is no harsher critic of Cleveland anywhere than a native son."

Cuyahoga County was growing, but only in the suburbs, which took more than population from the city. Outlying shopping centers had begun to take a fatal toll on downtown department stores. The region's first indoor shopping mall, Severance Center, was under construction in Cleveland Heights, promising "all of the 'Downtown' advantages, but with none of the bother."

Cleveland, the nation's fifth-largest city in the 1930 census, had fallen to eighth by 1960 and was dropping. White flight and block-busting were changing the complexion of East Side neighborhoods and touching inner-ring suburbs, while the city's large and growing black population—often displaced by redevelopment—was becoming its single largest ethnic segment. Race relations were deteriorating, but not as badly as they would a year later over the issue of *de facto* segregation.

A lot of white Clevelanders were still dealing with their own ethnicity. In a city founded by New Englanders as the Western Reserve of Connecticut, now one of every three residents had been born abroad or was a first-generation American, and sixty-three separate ethnic groups were identified on the mostly white West Side alone.

Cleveland was a stronghold of working-class "cosmos," especially Eastern Europeans, who defended their neighborhoods and homes, trimmed their lawns, and shoveled their walks. But to a younger generation, taking its cues from stylish Jack and Jackie in the White House, their babushkas and polkas were anachronisms at best and embarrassments at worst.

"Wide scale scorn for working-class ethnicity prevailed, particularly in the media," Joseph Valencic wrote, years later, in his entry about polkas in the *Encyclopedia of Cleveland History*. "Frankie Yankovic's comic hit 'Who Stole the Kishka?' was ridiculed as a prime example of ethnic low culture."

The daily newspapers that should have covered Cleveland in early 1963, the *Plain Dealer* and the *Cleveland Press*, were in the middle of a 129-day strike and shutdown that wouldn't end until April.

Broadcasting, already woven into the fabric of the community, came to occupy an even more vital place in its consciousness. Television, which had arrived only fifteen years earlier but which had quickly grown into the dominant broadcast medium, became for the first time a kind of lifeline for people huddled in their homes, watching the snow drift outside.

Cleveland radio in 1963 primarily meant a handful of AM stations. FM was still the rarefied province of longhairs, at a time when "longhair" still meant Beethoven and not four moptops from Liverpool.

BAXTER & RILEY,
WERE RADIO.

JACK RILEY

JEFF BAXTER

WJW Radio, once the raucous home of Alan Freed and Pete Myers, had settled into a middle-of-the-road format of pop standards with hosts like the bow-tied Ed Fisher and piano-playing Ronnie Barrett. WDOK had a similar easy-listening format, anchored in the morning by the venerable Tom Armstrong. WGAR's higher-brow programming included a heavy dose of news, network broadcasts, and the Metropolitan Opera. WERE's crazy-quilt schedule ranged from the morning show of grumpy Bob Neal, who teamed with Ken Coleman to announce Indians games on TV, through the comedy of Jeff Baxter and Jack Riley, to the nightly Catholic Rosary broadcast. WJMO and WABQ programmed rhythm and blues for the black community.

For young people, the platters that mattered were on WHK and KYW; those were the rock and roll outlets buzzing from the tinny transistors that had been arriving from Japan.

Top-rated WHK, "Color Channel 14," featured echo-chambered, fast-talking "Good Guys" like Johnny Holliday spinning hits from the station's record chart, the Fabulous 50 Tunedex, in the "glass cage" studio at 5000 Euclid Ave. KYW, almost stately by comparison, had "VIPs" like Specs

GHOULARDI
Chapter 4

"Who Stole The Kishka?"

Howard and Jim Runyon playing the Sound 11 Survey, on a signal that boomed at night to thirty-eight states.

Alan Freed, the pioneering deejay who had named the music "rock and roll" on his WJW "Moondog" show, had long since departed for greater fame and eventual disgrace in New York. He now was remembered mostly for the 1952 "Moondog Coronation Ball" that devolved into a riot at the oversold Cleveland Arena, and for being banished from New York airwaves over his role in radio's pay-for-play "payola" scandal in 1959.

That scandal had touched local personalities as well. Popular Joe Finan of KYW was one of those fired after admitting to a House subcommittee that he had accepted money from record companies to give special treatment to their releases.

Looking for a degree of respectability and even safety, stations found some of it in the musical trough that followed the turn of the decade. Buddy Holly, Richie Valens, and J. P. "Big Bopper" Richardson had died in a plane crash. Elvis had gone into the army, Little Richard had found religion, Chuck Berry had been busted, and Jerry Lee Lewis was banned from many stations after marrying his thirteen-year-old cousin.

"The big record companies got into the music and took over from the smaller, independent record labels," said Denny Sanders, program director of Cleveland oldies station WMJI-FM. "They created prefab, corporate rock stars, the Fabians and Frankie Avalons, who were more entertainers than originators. While they made some pretty enjoyable music, none of them would be considered true artists."

West Coast surf music and Barry Gordy's Motown sound were only beginning to stir. The Beatles were more than a year away from exploding in America on *The Ed Sullivan Show*.

At the top of the pops were smoothies like "Go Away Little Girl" by Steve Lawrence, "Hey Paula," by Paul & Paula, and "Walk Right In" by the Rooftop Singers. Paul Petersen of *The Donna Reed Show* was climbing the charts with "My Dad," following in the footsteps of TV sibling Shelley Fabares and her "Johnny Angel."

With Rick Nelson of *Ozzie & Harriet*, they were TV's standard-bearers

RALPH LOCHER HITS
A BUTTON TO SWITCH
ON WJW'S COLOR
BROADCASTING.

RALPH LOCHER HITS
A BUTTON TO SWITCH
ON WJW'S COLOR
BROADCASTING.

ROMPER ROOM'S
"MISS BARBARA,"
BARBARA PLUMMER.

PAIGE PALMER,
EXERCISE PRIESTESS.

GHOULARDI
Chapter 4

of a youth culture that found its major expression on *American Bandstand*, where well-groomed young people in skirts and ties demonstrated their wholesomeness.

A maturing Annette Funicello, stirring the libidos of young males who didn't know what a libido was, had traded her Mickey Mouse Club ears for a beach blanket in movies like *Beach Party*, in which an anthropologist studies "wild teens" like twenty-three-year-old Frankie Avalon.

Television in Cleveland consisted of three stations: KYW (Channel 3), WEWS (Channel 5), and WJW (Channel 8).

Congress had just passed a law requiring that TV sets be manufactured to receive the UHF signals above Channel 13, but it mattered little that most sets didn't yet have the capability: Cleveland's first UHF station, WVIZ (Channel 25), would not begin limited service as a National Educational Television outlet until 1965, and the first commercial UHF station, WKBF (Channel 61), would not arrive until 1968.

Most receivers were black-and-white, and so was most programming. Color programs were so rare—typically a half dozen a day on KYW—that they were designated with stars and boldface in listings. When WJW broadcast the city's first local program in color, in March 1964, Mayor Locher would be on hand to push the control-room button.

Evening newscasts ran only fifteen minutes. No-nonsense Bill Jorgensen anchored KYW's *Eyewitness News* with his signature sign-off, "Thanking you for your time, this time, until next time." Plummy-voiced radio veteran Tom Field read the news on WEWS, where Dorothy Fuldheim delivered nightly commentaries behind a desk bearing a Duquesne beer logo. Sincere young Doug Adair anchored *City Camera* on WJW, where Western Reserve University professor Warren Guthrie was about to end twelve years as the "Sohio Reporter."

But newscasts were only a small portion of the locally produced programming. Videotape and satellite feeds had not yet revolutionized syndication with fast, cheap program distribution, so live and local shows, as brief as five minutes and as long as ninety, were still the mainstay during hours when the networks were dark. They were a tradition born of necessity at WEWS, an ABC affiliate at a time when that network had no daytime schedule.

Barbara Plummer entertained tots on *Romper Room* every morning, while the leotard-clad host of *The Paige Palmer Show* dispensed beauty tips and performed calisthenics for their mothers—typically using "fanny bumps" to battle the scourge of "saddlebag thighs."

The 1 O'Clock Club, with an audience that sometimes seemed a sea of blue hair, featured interviews, book reviews, and the somewhat edgy banter of Fuldheim and Bill "Smoochie" Gordon, the gregarious, lip-smacking former radio deejay whose signature sign-off was "Stay smoochie, you rascal you."

Gene Carroll, a local radio star of the 1930s who went on to open a talent school on Euclid Avenue in the 1940s, was in his fifteenth year hosting a noontime Sunday amateur hour. *The Gene Carroll Show* spawned some local celebrities—fifteen-year-old protégé Andrea Carroll, no relation, sold 40,000 copies of her 1962 recording "Please Don't Talk to the Lifeguard"—but would be remembered as well for its dancers, lip-synchers, and "production numbers." It would also leave the memory of the skinny, jug-eared Carroll emerging to the strains of "Hold That Tiger"—music highlighting sponsor Giant Tiger, a chain of discount stores that challenged local blue laws to open on Sunday.

Carroll's show ran back-to-back with *Polka Varieties*—a local institution whose name, some maintained, was an inherent contradiction. Local and touring bands performed while a dancing audience jockeyed for camera position.

KYW, driven by the ambitions of owner Westinghouse Broadcasting, had taken aim at *The 1 O'Clock Club* with *The Mike Douglas Show*, and got a competitive jump by starting at 12:30 p.m. Douglas, previously a club singer, fronted a

GENE CARROLL (WITH ANDREA CARROLL).

POLKA VARIETIES.

BILL "SMOOCHIE" GORDON AND DOROTHY FULDHEIM ON THE SET OF THEIR 1 O'CLOCK CLUB SHOW AT THE START OF THE SIXTH SEASON IN 1962.

The Best Location

more contemporary ninety-minute talk and variety show that featured music from the Ellie Frankel Trio, and a different celebrity co-host each week.

WJW was trying to imitate Douglas with *Dale Young Time*, a little-remembered, bargain-basement knockoff that featured a singing host and was cancelled after thirty weeks. The station aimed for kids with "B'wana Don" Hunt in the morning, but found far more success with Jim Doney's *Adventure Road*, a long-running afternoon show built around guests presenting films about exotic locales.

The shows for young people were generally shows for the youngest people. Two would be remembered above all by the postwar "baby boomers" who, by 1963, were starting to outgrow them.

Linn Sheldon—a versatile local TV pioneer who had lip-synched records on Cleveland's first sponsored program at WEWS and hosted more than thirty shows in forty-three years on the air—ruled afternoons as Barnaby, the straw-hatted, pointy-eared leprechaun character he launched on KYW in 1957. He entertained several generations of "little neighbors" and their parents with whimsical humor, life lessons, and cartoons, and he had enough skill as a ventriloquist to supply the voice of Long John, his invisible parrot. He once drew a crowd of 8,000 small-fry and their "invisible pets" for a downtown parade, and each of them was sure his signature sign-off was meant for them personally: "If anybody calls, tell them Barnaby says hello. And tell them that I think that you are the nicest person in the whole world—just you."

BARNABY AND FANS.

KIDDIE-SHOW HOST CAPTAIN PENNY (RON PENFOUND) WITH "MISS BARBARA" PLUMMER OF ROMPER ROOM.

Tall and lanky host Ron Penfound could draw a slightly older crowd to WEWS each afternoon as railroader Captain Penny, thanks to the drawing power of his Three Stooges one-reelers. Since the Stooges drew wrathful mail from parents and teachers, the Captain always reminded kids not to imitate them—while always announcing them as "Larry, Curly, and Moe," an order that viewers who ventured beyond Cleveland were surprised to find was not a universal litany. He also hosted unpredictable animal segments featuring pets from the Animal Protective League ("Pooch Parade") and more exotic offerings from "Jungle Larry" Tetzlaff and his wife, "Safari Jane."

Youngsters knew the Captain's daily walkaway by heart: "You can fool some of the people all of the time, all of the people some of the time, but you can't fool mom. She's pretty nice and she's pretty smart—you listen to her and you won't go far wrong."

Penfound's story would become one of the sadder chapters in local broadcasting. His death from cancer, at age forty-seven in 1974, came exactly

GHOULARDI

Chapter 4

"If anybody calls, tell them Barnaby says hello."

ten years after his second wife, Phyllis, jumped to her death from the Cuyahoga River Bridge of the Ohio Turnpike. She was said to be despondent and in ill health, and Clevelanders reacted to the front-page news of her suicide as they might to a death in the family.

In fact, the behind-the-scenes reality of broadcasting was frequently less rosy than what the audience perceived. Hard living and hard drinking were common among performers of the era, and sometimes took a toll on lives and careers that fell short of expectations.

Few, if any, partied harder or drank more than Linn Sheldon, who finally gave it up in 1974. His subsequent work helping others surmount alcoholism would become a legacy equal to the better-known memory of Barnaby.

"They say if you have two drinks a day, it helps you live longer," he said. "Well, by the time I was fifty-five, I had had enough drinks to live to be 3,000. I decided that was enough."

But the dark lining rarely showed through the silver-cloud image of local television: wholesome, authoritative, trustworthy, and neighborly.

No less than its natives, Ernie Anderson was ambivalent about Cleveland.

"I think he was real happy about the popularity he had in Cleveland," Bob Soinski said, "but he came from Massachusetts, that's where he was born."

Thirty-five years after Ernie left New England, Boston continued to draw him on spring and fall pilgrimages, and his enthusiasm for that city never waned. He called it "the best city in the entire country" and a "wonderful, wonderful town."

Cleveland, on the other hand, alternately disappointed him and embraced him, scolded and celebrated him. He reveled in it and chafed against it.

ABOVE: WOODROW THE WOODSMAN AND BARNABY.

SELECTED LOCAL TV SHOWS, 1963

Adventure Road, travel films, hosted by Jim Doney. Began on Saturdays in 1962, later daily.

Barnaby, Popeye and Friends, daily kids' fare hosted by Linn "Barnaby" Sheldon.

B'wana Don, daily children's show with "B'wana Don" Hunt and the chimpanzee Bongo Bailey.

Dale Young Time, short-lived daily talk/variety show.

5 O'Clock Show, also known as *Captain Penny's Clubhouse,* daily cartoons and kiddie fare hosted by Ron "Captain Penny" Penfound.

The Gene Carroll Show, Sunday variety show and amateur showcase.

The Mike Douglas Show, daily live talk-variety show.

1 O'Clock Club, daily talk hosted by Bill Gordon and Dorothy Fuldheim.

Paige Palmer Show, daily exercise.

Polka Varieties, Sunday-afternoon music series.

Quarterback Club, weekly Browns highlight show during football season, hosted by Ken Coleman.

Romper Room, daily show hosted in Cleveland by "Miss Barbara" Plummer.

Woodrow, daily children's show with Woodrow the Woodsman (Clay Conroy).

GHOULARDI
The Best Location

**GHOULARDI DRUMS UP
SUPPORT FOR AN
INDIANS HOME OPENER.**

"It wasn't really my kind of . . . country," he said in a 1990 interview for *The Plain Dealer*.

A harsher judgment came at the prodding of interviewer Scott Eyman for an *Ohio Magazine* article in 1978.

"I remember they said that I was too sophisticated for the kids," Ernie said. "I'm not too hip, Cleveland's too square. Cleveland is a dreadful place, full of petty, narrow, little people. It's a mirror for industrial cities. They're all going to be like that, and they've just staved it off a little longer than Cleveland has.

"But Cleveland, man, waves after waves of uneducated working-class people. After the Hungarian revolution, Cleveland was a reasonable town for a lot of refugees. It didn't overwhelm them and they could find work. In Boston they'd have starved to death, but in Cleveland they could earn a living."

Talking with Chuck Schodowski a decade later, he was mellower and more reflective on the same subject.

"I don't know whether I could have succeeded with the Ghoulardi thing anyplace other than Cleveland, because [there] was such an ethnic disparity, all kinds of people," he said. "I could do all kinds of things and get to all kinds of people. I didn't hold off on anything. I had a really good time in Cleveland.

"Cleveland's what you make it," he said. "If you have great friends, as I did, you can have a great time in Cleveland."

"He liked Cleveland," Tim Conway said without hesitation. "We enjoyed Cleveland together. We did a lot of things together. He and I were together eighteen, twenty hours a day and weekends, we were very, very good friends. He enjoyed my humor and I enjoyed his, and we enjoyed putting Cleveland on, in a sense."

Had the Ghoulardi show or some version of *Ernie's Place* ever reached syndication, Conway said, "I don't know that he ever would have wanted to leave Cleveland."

His influence never did leave, at least for that generation of kids who watched him during their formative years.

P.J. Bednarski, editor of the national weekly *Electronic Media* and former TV critic for newspapers including *USA Today* and the *Chicago Sun-Times*, grew up amid Ghoulardimania in suburban Garfield Heights.

"Every person from that era whom I've talked to—every guy, at least—each acknowledges in his own way how Ghoulardi was somebody who gave them an attitude about life at that point that was something that stuck to them," he said. "You didn't take things the way you were supposed to. You were cool and sort of bemused by the passing scene and what was going on in society. You were satirically scornful of it. Martin Mull's comedy, I think, was an extension of Ghoulardi in a way. You made fun of what you were supposed to take reverentially, including yourself.

"It was disobedient," Bednarski said. "If you were thirteen or fourteen, it was fascinating to see you could be disobedient and make it. It's now very regular to make fun of another media person, but it was very risky stuff then. It was very underground.

"It was the first time you'd ever seen television, or any medium, that you knew was outside what it was supposed to be doing. That if the general manager ever saw it, he'd yank it off the air."

Ernie also made fun of Cleveland itself, a place that seemed somehow bigger and more important than it would a decade later, but that still retained the sensibilities of a smaller town.

"Cleveland has always had a sense of humor about itself, sometimes to its detriment," Bednarski said. The attitude was tough, but more ironic than cynical. It could be self-mocking, and it was aimed most sharply at any sort of pretension.

"Ghoulardi was amazingly self-deprecatory in a way that is kind of Cleveland," Bednarski said. "It's like the T-shirts from the '70s and '80s: 'Cleveland: Too Tough To Die.' 'Cleveland: You've Gotta Be Tough.' Ghoulardi was emblematic of that sort of attitude.

"Cleveland is also Middle America," Bednarski said, which meant Ghoulardi didn't have to aim at big sacred cows to cause a stir. "To be irreverent about a manicured lawn was perfectly anti-establishment."

NAMES ON THE NEWS

News watchers in the early 1960s could see anchors Warren Guthrie, Tom Field, and Bill Jorgensen; weather forecasters Dick Goddard, Carolyn Johnson, and Howard Hoffmann; sports anchor John Fitzgerald; commentators Norman Wagy and Dorothy Fuldheim; and "city reporter" Doug Adair.

"Cleveland: You've Gotta Be Tough."

GHOULARDI
The Best Location

The Monster That Devoured Cleveland

On **The Many Loves of Dobie Gillis**, TV's original beatnik, Maynard G. Krebs, often named a fictitious horror movie, **The Monster That Devoured Cleveland**, as his favorite film.

In real life, the monster that devoured the city was the beatnik horror host known as Ghoulardi . . .

GHOULARDI
The Monster That Devoured Cleveland

Ghoulardi hit Cleveland with a bigger blast than all of the fireworks he used on the air. In fact, many describe the show's impact in pyrotechnic terms—it was "like a skyrocket," according to Bob Soinski.

"It absolutely exploded," said Tim Conway.

"Ernie was probably the biggest thing ever to hit Cleveland."

The ratings proved it, and for WJW—like all TV stations—the ratings were the ultimate gauge of popular success or failure. The ratings measured the size of the viewing audience, through telephone surveys and viewer diaries, and determined whether sponsors would buy commercial time on a show or shun it.

A hot show meant money, and Ghoulardi was on fire.

The American Research Bureau, whose Arbitron service had long been the gold standard in Cleveland, found that WJW's late Friday movie averaged a 7 rating before Ghoulardi, meaning it was watched in seven percent of homes in Greater Cleveland. In ARB's measurements for March-April 1963, the first to include *Shock Theater,* WJW soared to a 20 rating—three times as many homes, in less than three months.

The competing A. C. Nielsen Company reported similar results. By its count, WJW's late movie averaged a 10.9 rating in the weeks before Ghoulardi, and immediately jumped to a 16 rating for the first month that included *Shock Theater.* The rating climbed to 19.4 the next month, and 20.7 the month after that.

The numbers came close to those racked up by network hits among the Top Twenty-five in prime-time evening hours. By the standards of late-night hours, when fewer people watch TV, they were nothing short of astonishing.

Even more dramatic were Nielsen's share-of-audience evaluations, which measure a program's performance in relation to direct competition —in other words, how big a proportion of the audience pie it gets. By the spring of 1963, Ghoulardi on Friday nights commanded an astounding 56-percent share of the late-night audience, compared to a 38 share for Johnny Carson and a 6 share for Steve Allen. Local TV veterans, recalling long-lost ratings reports, are probably not exaggerating when they insist that *Shock*

HOWARD HOFFMANN
DOES THE WEATHER IN
GHOULARDI GETUP.

GHOULARDI
Chapter 5

Theater on occasion captured upwards of 70 percent of the late-night audience.

WJW, which usually rated second or third among Cleveland's three stations over the course of a whole broadcast week, was boosted to first overall on the strength of Ghoulardi.

Cleveland police added a unique testimonial of their own.

"They informed us that crime on Friday night was far lower than any other night," Schodowski said, "and they attributed it to everybody watching Ghoulardi." One figure, commonly cited at the time, held that juvenile crime dropped thirty-five percent during the show.

Laughing about the unstated significance of the statistic years later, Jack Riley said, "You know what Ernie's audience was, then—hoodlums, thieves . . ."

Ernie, who claimed he "truthfully never really saw the [audience] shares," modestly offered a more mordant assessment of the dip in Cleveland's crime rate in that first Ghoulardi winter. "Nobody likes to steal a car in a blizzard," he said.

By May 1963, the national show-business newspaper *Variety* was calling Ghoulardi "the hottest property in town." WJW, though at first bewildered and uneasy with his success, was soon ready to milk it for all it was worth.

On April 13, 1963, the station gave him a second weekly movie show, *Masterpiece Theater*, at 6:00 p. m. Saturday. *Cleveland Press* "Showtime" writer Jim Frankel thought Ernie was already "in danger of overdoing the bit," but also noted that he cannily modified the presentation to fit an earlier time period and younger audience.

On Fridays, Ghoulardi appeared before a dark background in dramatic bottom-lit facial closeup. On *Masterpiece Theater*, a less intimidating and more brightly lit Ghoulardi was seen at a greater distance, often sitting in a chair before a backdrop of drawings and posters that expanded into a painted castle.

Ernie's instincts were on target. His hip Friday show had become a cult ritual among teenage viewers and a week-ending habit among the adults who—perhaps surprisingly—formed the biggest portion of his audience by far. The Saturday show put him into schoolyards and a new stratosphere of attention.

PROMOTIONAL MATERIAL FOR ERNIE, 1963.

GHOULARDI
The Monster That Devoured Cleveland

Sponsor magazine, a TV-radio trade publication, spelled out Ghoulardi's appeal as measured by ratings services. The Friday show was typically watched by 130,000 men, 155,000 women, 104,000 teens and, remarkably, 61,200 children, for a total audience of 450,200 people.

The Saturday show drew a smaller audience of 389,000, including 67,000 men, 84,000 women, and 100,000 teens. But many of those were new viewers who didn't stay up on Friday night. More significantly, they were augmented by the 138,000 children who were watching—more than double the Friday number.

A few months after his debut, Ghoulardi ranked behind only the long-running Barnaby in a survey of schoolchildren asked to name their favorite broadcast personalities by the Radio-TV Council of Greater Cleveland.

If WJW's management needed more tangible proof of Ghoulardimania, they only needed to ask the post office.

In less than three months, 10,000 pieces of mail poured into the station. Ernie's casual remark one day about a non-existent "Ghoulgateers Club" drew more than 3,000 letters alone. By summer, Ghoulardi was getting some 4,000 pieces of mail a week. Ernie's basement office, the size of a large closet, bulged with it.

GHOULARDI WITH "COOL-IT BOX," A SMALL MOTORIZED FAN.

"The reaction is fantastic," he said. "It's like 1948 television all over again," referring to a time, only fifteen years earlier, when TV was like a fresh canvas and anything touching it made a noticeable impression.

"There was so much mail no one could even open it all," Soinski recalled. "One day the fire inspector came in and ordered all this stuff cleared out, because it became a fire hazard."

The mail wasn't limited to letters—or to the customary fan tributes of homemade posters and drawings.

There was a "Last Aid Kit" bearing the advice, "Don't take Bufferin, take a fink drink." There was a Ghoulitar, a guitar with an extra hole in it. There were shirts and hats inscribed with greetings, paper fans, electric fans, a battery-powered, shock-inducing "Cool-It Kit" and a "Kick Me" football helmet with an electric light attachment.

Kids sent in model cars and especially favored those with the imprint of California customizer Ed "Big Daddy" Roth, who had a Ghoulardi-like goatee and a "Rat Fink" mascot. It might have seemed cruel to adults when Ghoulardi blew up one of the offerings with a firecracker, but not to the kids.

"They didn't care," Ernie said. "They were proud of it. They wanted me to blow them up."

Kids didn't merely send more models—they sent some with built-in firecrackers, ready for detonation.

The mail brought homemade cannons, "Ghoul Scout" cookies and

TIME WAS NOT ON HIS SIDE

GHOULARDI HAD BEEN ON THE AIR BARELY EIGHT MONTHS WHEN TIME MAGAZINE BROUGHT HIM TO THE ATTENTION OF THE NATION.

In its "Education" department, of all places, under the sub-heading of "Students," the newsweekly's edition of September 27, 1963 carried a report that was admirably complete but not admiring in tone. It appeared under the headline "What Catches the Teen-age Mind," and was accompanied by a photo captioned, "Cleveland's Ghoulardi: A deity for teendom tedium."

"The teen-age imagination is hard to catch," it began, "but once caught, easy to cage. Someone who calls himself Ghoulardi has caged nearly every teen-age mind in Cleveland.

"He is both host and intruder on a daily series of old one-reel comedies on WJW-TV. He wears a pointed, Satanic goatee, trick glasses and a horned hairdo—in the understandable hope that the adult community will not recognize him as Ernie Anderson, erstwhile announcer of commercials for power companies and banks."

The story went on to describe Ghoulardi's appearance and basic routine, mentioned some ghoul-ish puns and catchwords ("High school teachers hold spelling bees between Knifs and Ghoulardis") and recounted how Ghoulardi "intrudes himself into the old movies he hosts."

It concluded: "There is a widespread canard that 1963's teen-agers are brighter, quicker, and of higher intellectual potential attainment than any previous generation. Ghoulardi has knocked that theory into a cocked hat. Or rather into a football helmet with faucets sticking out of it. He wears one. Zow."

---

cakes, Ghoul Easter eggs, cardboard skeletons, a three-foot butterfly, a Knif Killer, a Knifometer, and a bloody hand.

The bloody hand was fake. But the dog skull was real, as were the live white mice, the live snake (delivered in person), an alligator, dead goldfish, dead bees, and a dead bat on a string.

There was a live crow, whose exact origin remains cloudy.

"I think Ernie borrowed it," Schodowski said. "It wasn't surprising, he'd bring anything in."

Ernie named the crow Oxnard, for the southern California city whose name he would periodically invoke—"Remember: Oxnard!"—as an all-purpose catchword on his show. He had seen the name on a freeway sign during a trip to Los Angeles, Schodowski recalled, and said, "That's the dumbest name for a city I've ever heard in my life."

Oxnard the crow presented new possibilities.

"He was trying to get it to sit on his shoulder, which would have made a great visual," Schodowski said. "But it flew up into the rafters in the studio and perched above Jim Doney's set."

Doney was host of *Adventure Road*, the daily travel-movie show that was, like most local programs, broadcast live. Oxnard perched out of camera range but directly above his head.

ADVENTURE ROAD'S JIM DONEY.

GHOULARDI

The Monster That Devoured Cleveland

THE GHOULARDI
SWEATSHIRT.

FOR THE WELL-DRESSED
FAN: GHOULARDI BUTTONS.

RIGHT:
MANNERS' TAKE-HOME
HOT GHOULARDI CUP
WITH SEE-THROUGH
BOTTOM AND A
SEASONALLY ADJUSTED
CATCHPHRASE:
"HEAT IT, GROUP!"

Chapter 5

"Jim would be introducing his guests and talking, and all of a sudden you'd see his eyes flicker," Ernie recalled. "Because, you know how birds are—they have no control, is the word I think we're looking for, and you never know when. It could be, you come down [to the studio] and you gotta have the chair all washed and taken care of. I never understood why they didn't move the chair," he said. "Just move it over."

Schodowski recalls no ill will resulting from Oxnard's antics, and Doney later appeared on the Ghoulardi show in a skit featuring Ernie as a hilariously boring guest in an *Adventure Road* parody.

("This a field, Jim," Ernie said in earnest enthusiasm as Doney dozed off. "Right there is a cow. You know, we get milk from cows, Jim!")

But Chris Quinn is among those who remember when Oxnard's bombing led to fireworks. Quinn, the Cleveland disc jockey who periodically memorialized Ghoulardi on his WMJI-FM oldies show, was a fan who frequently visited WJW as a teenager with a friend whose father worked for the station.

"We had just walked in and we heard all this commotion and yelling," he said. "Here comes Ernie running through the lobby and out the door, being chased by Doney, who was beet red and screaming at the top of his lungs. It's a good thing Doney was short and stocky or he would have beaten the crap out of him."

It all ended after about a week, when Oxnard returned to his cage from the rafters.

"Probably got hungry," Ernie said. "He belonged to a priest, I found out, and the priest finally came and got him. I was really glad to get rid of him.

"I always have a feeling that birds like that, with those beaks, they think that's a grape," he added, poking a finger at Schodowski's eye. "They're gonna go, whap! any minute now—they're gonna pop that grape right out."

Management was glad to see Oxnard grounded, but gladder that Ghoulardi's popularity showed no sign of coming down to earth.

WJW's promotion department, led by Sheldon Saltman, talked to a bottling company about marketing a soft drink called "Ghoul-Aid" in Greater Cleveland, and to a novelty company about selling bouncing rubber skulls.

"Ghoul-Aid" fizzled, but other promotions popped—especially at Manners restaurants, the local chain that was the "Home of the Big Boy" and the place where carhops roamed in the days

before fastfood walk-up and drive-thru windows.

Early in the summer of 1963, Manners began featuring the Big Ghoulardi milkshake, a sickly blue and green concoction in an orange take-home cup. For winter, the menu added the Hot Ghoulardi Cup, an apple-cider drink in a take-home mug with a see-through bottom and Ghoulardi's image on the side. Manners also distributed bumper stickers with the drinks (green for the shake, orange for the Hot Ghoulardi) and green Ghoulardi bookcovers for "ghoul books."

Grocery stores rang up $60,000 in sales of Ghoulardi "Stay Sick" sweatshirts in the late summer and fall of 1963; Ernie's cut was twenty percent.

Others also tried to cash in on the mania that extended to "Stay Sick" buttons and Ghoulardi sunglasses.

Most notable was Ernest Anderson of Shaker Heights—no relation to Ernie, but about the same age—who found himself thrust into unwelcome celebrity through his namesake. He hit the newspapers in August 1963 after appearing in Shaker Heights Municipal Court on charges of intoxication and disturbing the peace.

Anderson blamed his plight on a plague of late-night phone calls from Ghoulardi fans telling him to "stay sick" and "turn blue" before hanging up. Municipal Judge John Corlett, saying he had heard some weird excuses on the bench, fined Anderson $100 but sympathetically suspended it, leaving him to pay $11 in court costs.

Anderson subsequently incorporated a company under the name Ghoulardi Inc., naming himself as president. He said he intended to sell clothing and novelties with Ghoulardi's name and picture to annoy WJW.

Storer Broadcasting, arguing that the firm sought to profit from WJW's exclusive property, filed suit in September and won a temporary restraining order in Common Pleas Court. A month later, Judge Saul Danaceau ruled Ghoulardi Inc. out of business.

TOP: THE HOT GHOULARDI DRINK AND ITS STICKER WENT FOR 40 CENTS.

MIDDLE: FOR 35 CENTS, MANNERS PATRONS GOT A BIG GHOULARDI DRINK PLUS A STICKER.

BOTTOM: MANNERS' GREEN, PROOF-OF-PURCHASE BIG GHOULARDI BUMPER STICKER.

GHOULARDI
The Monster That Devoured Cleveland

There was no room for interlopers anyway—not the way WJW was milking Ghoulardi.

On July 15, 1963, the station again expanded his on-air duties and aimed more directly at kids with *Laurel, Ghoulardi and Hardy,* a half-hour show at 5:00 p.m., Monday through Friday. Ernie again toned down his act, in keeping with the afternoon hour and old-time comedy, but even a tamer version of the character seemed subversive to some parents of the children at whom it was aimed.

As far as they were concerned, the world would end not with a bang, or a boom-boom, but a whisker.

"Among Ghoulardi's critics—and there are many if my mail is an indicator—it's common to dismiss the man as one who appeals only to youngsters and to condemn him for corrupting their taste," wrote *Cleveland Press* TV critic Bill Barrett.

It was the era when "dead baby jokes" made the rounds in playgrounds and schoolyards, when *Mad* magazine was making subversive sport of politicians and societal conventions, and when schools were instructing kids how to "duck and cover" against a Soviet atomic attack .

Plain Dealer TV editor Bert J. Reesing saw Ghoulardi as a purveyor of "shock programming" whose "demonic antics" would have a negative psychological effect on impressionable young minds. Another *Plain Dealer* writer thought the show was "aimed at the Neanderthal mind," and that its popularity "must rank—no pun intended—among the great unsolved mysteries of the ages."

Even the national newsweekly *Time* jumped into the fray, calling Ghoulardi "a deity for teendom tedium."

"There were a lot of letters from people wanting to get him off [the air] because he was a bad influence on children," Jack Riley said. "He was nuts."

He was also more visible than ever, starring in seven shows a week.

Even the Three Stooges (the final troupe of Moe Howard, Larry Fine, and "Curly Joe" DeRita) paid a respectful visit to the show, though their classic short films were a staple on *Captain Penny's Clubhouse* over on WEWS.

The appearance was recalled by Robert Benjamin, who grew up in Parma Heights and knew the Stooges through the old friendship between his mother, Jean, and Curly Joe, whom she later married. "When the Stooges were booked to be on *Ghoulardi*, someone at the station wanted them to steal the show away from him" in order to take Ernie down a peg, Benjamin said. "Joe said, 'We know we're guests, we're not going to do that, it's not right.' So they were more low key than they otherwise might have been."

In September, WJW shifted the weekday show to 4:30 p.m. and started

Ernie *Interviews* Ghoulardi

ANNOUNCER ERNIE ANDERSON ONCE PLAYED STRAIGHT MAN TO HIS ALTER EGO GHOULARDI IN AN INTERVIEW. THE TWO IMAGES WERE SET SIDE BY SIDE AT A NEWS ANCHOR DESK, ERNIE IN HIS SUIT ON THE RIGHT, GHOULARDI ON THE LEFT WITH HIS WIG, BUTTON-COVERED VEST, AND BEARD.

ERNIE: Good evening, Ernie Anderson here. We'd like tonight to interview probably one of the most outstanding personalities in the Cleveland area, and maybe of our time: Ghoulardi. And I'm sure it's going to be a lot of laughs. Mr. Ghoulardi-- may I call you Ghoulardi?

GHOULARDI: No, as a matter of fact. You may call me Mr. Ghoulardi, or King.

ERNIE: What do you want me to call you?

GHOULARDI: I just told you. King.

ERNIE: Oh, well, King--

GHOULARDI: King.

ERNIE: --could you tell us when you first got your start as Ghoulardi?

GHOULARDI: I first got my start when they fired me from Channel 3 and 5 wouldn't hire me.

ERNIE: Could you tell us to what you owe the success of Ghoulardi?

GHOULARDI: I owe the success of Ghoulardi to my outstanding talent. (squawks)

ERNIE: It has been rumored that you are seeing Dorothy.

GHOULARDI: Oh, no. That's an outrageous lie. I never could see her. (laughs) Hey, you some

kind of announcer, kid? Why don't you do an ID?

ERNIE: Well, if I can.

GHOULARDI: Go ahead. You can do it.

ERNIE: I'd be happy to. (voice deepens) WJW-TV, Cleveland.

GHOULARDI: Well, that stinks. Could you introduce the show?

ERNIE: And now, the Ghoulardi show--

GHOULARDI: Ahh!

ERNIE: Or the King show.

GHOULARDI: King, right. Hey, why don't you touch up your sideburns? You kind of ugly on the tube. You look like you got a haircut in Parma.

talking about syndicating it to other cities, getting a backhanded boost when *Time* magazine reported in October that "Ghoulardi has caged nearly every teen-age mind in Cleveland."

"Surely the local television business has never seen anything quite like Ghoulardi and his amazing, if somewhat unexplainable, success," Barrett wrote in the *Press*, admitting, "I personally can't explain it" and "I don't dig the message."

Ernie, who dug it but couldn't explain it, told Barrett he could keep the mania going "for another five years with no trouble at all."

But the weekday show proved to be a drain on his energy that also failed to dent the ratings dominance of *Barnaby* on KYW.

Even so, WJW tried to keep it going when Ernie and other performers in the American Federation of Television and Radio Artists (AFTRA) went on strike in November over talent fees and working conditions. While Ernie walked a picket line outside, Storer's program development manager, Bob Guy, and WJW staff artist Lionel Van Timmons served as replacement Ghoulardis, donning beards, glasses, lab coats, and hats to imitate his routines.

They substituted on a Saturday and four of the weekday shows. The fifth daily show, and their second weekend, were canceled by coverage of the JFK assassination on November 22.

The strike was settled the following week, and *Laurel, Ghoulardi and Hardy* was dropped as of December 9—a victim of forces that included WJW's peculiar, host-exhausting plans for syndication.

On November 11, Ernie had started doing a half-hour show at 4:00 p.m. weekdays for WSPD-TV, WJW's Storer-owned sister station in Toledo. But even by the standards of the 1960s, when instantaneous satellite transmission had not yet replaced the big reels of film or videotape that were couriered from station to station around the country, it was not really syndication at all.

Ernie did a separate production for WSPD. He would drive alone to Toledo each Tuesday, tape five shows, and drive back to Cleveland on Wednesday morning. Worse, he was coming cold to an unfamiliar market without his safety net of cronies.

"I don't dig the message."

—BILL BARRETT, CLEVELAND PRESS TV CRITIC

"I had to ask people who the local heavies were who were susceptible to the shaft," he told *Monsterscene* magazine. "It was tough to do. I was working off the hip. There was no help and no writers. They'd say, 'OK, Ernie, it's station break time. Go!' I've got nowhere to go. I can't think of a thing.

"I was improvising all the time, with the exception of some of those 16mm filmed openings we used to do for WJW. If I could get a news cameraman to take time from the women's club meeting or whatever and come film with me and do my little sketch, I'd be real lucky. I'd have to direct it and create it off the top of my head so I'd know it would get together. It was all on the fly."

The enterprise was probably doomed from the start. Instead of horror movies or old comedy one-reelers, Ghoulardi hosted *Maverick* reruns on WSPD. Station management tied his hands further by telling him to go easy on knocking the TV competition.

In January, approaching the end of his thirteen-week trial run, he was canceled in Toledo.

Ghoulardi, Ernie concluded, "was a very regional concept."

Very regional. In Cleveland, Ghoulardi was King, as he had proclaimed himself, and his influence spread beyond TV.

Because Ernie played it and fans demanded it, record distributors started ordering copies of "Papa-Oom-Mow-Mow" by the Rivingtons, the R&B novelty record that hadn't cracked the top thirty after it was released in 1962. Re-released in Northeast Ohio, the record reached No. 1 on the WHK Tunedex on September 30, 1963, and held its position for seven weeks.

Rock and roll disc jockeys, hoping to capture some of Ghoulardi's antic flair, started slipping polkas into their shows, sometimes inviting "make it or break it" phone calls from listeners.

Ghoulardi was so ubiquitous that he even seemed to be where he was

**RON SWEED, AS
ERNIE MET HIM.**

not. A lot of kids thought Bobby Vinton's singing of the words "heartache on heartache," in his summer 1963 hit "Blue on Blue," sounded suspiciously like "Harley, Ghoulardi."

At the invitation of a producer in New York, Ernie even recorded his own novelty record, "The Ghoulardi Surf," which was designed to be played from the inside out. It was never released, and Ron Sweed has what may be the only copy. Reminiscent of both the Surfaris' instrumental "Wipe Out" and *Mad* magazine's paperboard novelty record, "It's a Gas," "Ghoulardi Surf" opens with Ernie saying, "Hey group, cool it, ova dey," before a repeating falsetto chorus starts an endless chorus of "Stay sick, turn blue" and a twangy electric guitar takes over. Ernie delivers a few more catchphrases—"You won't believe," "I think we're in a lot of trouble," "The whole world's a purple knif"—before concluding, "Well, that stinks."

In person, Ghoulardi became the city's biggest crowd-pleaser. Only three weeks after his Saturday show started, Ernie recalled in a 1990 interview in *The Plain Dealer*, he was invited to make an appearance at the Cleveland Zoo, to climb the rocks at Monkey Island.

"There were so many kids at the field, we couldn't even get in there," he said. "They surrounded the car. I couldn't get out. I'll never forget that; I couldn't believe it."

In July, he paid a visit to Euclid Beach Park, the vintage amusement park that operated until 1969 along the Lake Erie shoreline on Cleveland's East Side. One of the fans who came to meet him was Ron Sweed, a thirteen-year-old from Forest Park Junior High School in Euclid, who arrived in a gorilla suit, led on a dog leash by a friend.

"Ernie couldn't believe I was stupid enough to wear a gorilla suit in the ninety-degree July heat," Sweed said, but there was a purpose to his mania. Meeting Ernie was the goal he had set for himself that year.

"I methodically set out to do it, and it worked," he said. "The minute he was on TV we were crazy about him. It didn't matter what was happening on Friday night. My friends and I would meet at someone's house to watch Ghoulardi. Everything else was secondary."

Sweed had lifted the gorilla suit from the props at a triple-feature horror matinee weeks earlier. Figuring it was his entree to Ernie, he put it on and rode the bus to Euclid Beach.

Ernie spotted him in the crowd while on stage for the first of three shows that mostly found him plugging park attractions, his own TV show, and the

"Get back, you wild beast!"

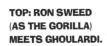

new Big Ghoulardi drink at Manners—"If it don't make you sick, you got a bad one!" He stopped cold at the sight of the gorilla, immediately seeing new possibilities, and summoned Sweed onstage.

"I don't beLIEVE dat ova dey!" he shouted. "Come on up, baby! Ghoulardi's gorilla, boys and girls! Get back, you wild beast!"

Ernie started improvising a gorilla-taming act, until Sweed backed a step too far and fell off the stage onto his back. Through the eye slits in the costume, he saw Ernie peering over the edge, laughing, "You OK ova dey, baby?"

Sweed clambered back up, followed Ernie to his toolshed "dressing room," got the autograph he wanted, and raced home to watch clips of himself that afternoon on *Laurel, Ghoulardi and Hardy*.

But Sweed saw himself as more than a fan. He returned to Euclid Beach for Ernie's two evening shows, again went on stage, and then persuaded his father to drive him to WJW the next day in time for *Masterpiece Theater*.

Once again, the gorilla suit was his entree. After a friendly security guard told Ernie of his presence, Sweed was invited to the studio, put on the air, and then allowed to hang around. He started showing up every week.

Though the gorilla suit lost its novelty for Ernie, Sweed struck a deal to wear it around the Manners restaurant near Euclid Beach. He was paid in food and promotional items but figured he was "doing my bit to keep Ghoulardi going."

At WJW, Sweed looked around and thought he could become an asset. Unpaid but unabashedly in awe of Ernie, he became a valuable gofer around the studio and office, helping with props, bringing some order to the mounds of mail, and befriending Ernie's oldest son, Michael.

"The office was just piled with stuff," Sweed said. "Not just Ghoulardi mail—stuff from ad agencies where he was doing freelance stuff. There'd be

TOP: RON SWEED (AS THE GORILLA) MEETS GHOULARDI.

BOTTOM: PROFILE OF A YOUNG RON SWEED.

GHOULARDI
The Monster That Devoured Cleveland

GHOULARDI'S MAIL

"Dear Ghoulardi: We love you. You're so different. Drop dead. Here's something that doesn't work. Hatefully, David Jones, 10."

"Dear Ghoulardi: You're awful! I don't know how my little girl can like you so much. Please send her a picture. Yours truly, Melissa Ann, 9-1/2."

"Dear Mr. Ghoulardy: Like many Clevelanders, we enjoy Channel 8's science fiction movies. Please try to be less obtrusive. Thanks, Steve."

"REGARDING GHOULARDI'S SHOW. SAME STINKS. SHOW GOOD. NOT THE NUT. WRITTEN BY THE ADULTS."

"It's not that he's handsome. It's that, well, he's just a great person."—Donna Myers of Lincoln High School, quoted in the *Cleveland Press*, 1963

checks four and five months old I'd put aside for him. 'Well, look at that! I thought they stiffed me! They did pay me! Thanks, Rawhn.'"

Sweed's duties, ever expanding as he began also showing up on weekdays after school, extended to booking personal appearances.

" . . . I had to finally ask him, when I was learning the ropes, because people would ask when they wanted to commission him for appearances: 'Mr. Anderson, they want to know what you do.' He said, 'What do I do? Tell 'em I show up!'

"I said, 'Is that what you want me to tell them, Mr. Anderson?' 'Damn right! I show up! Get the check and split!' I'd tell them, 'Mr. Anderson says he shows up.' Eventually, as I did it more, I said, 'Well, he'll sign autographs. . . . ' But he didn't sign too many. It was amazing the way he did things."

Ernie was invited to schools, fairs, parades, shopping centers, theater openings—anywhere a crowd might gather. He also began putting his appearances to work raising money for a variety of good causes.

Michael Weldon, writing in *Psychotronic* magazine, remembered Ghoulardi hosting a "Thrill Show" at Lakewood Civic Auditorium one Sunday afternoon, screening horror movies for the benefit of the Lakewood Junior Chamber of Commerce scholarship fund: "He introduced the movie *The Thing* and invited some kids with signs (including me) on stage. One of them brought firecrackers and got away with lighting them on the same stage that I later graduated on."

Out of costume and out on the street, Ernie cut an unimposing figure—pigeon-toed, shuffling along with his head down and hands jammed in his pockets. Ghoulardi turned him into the drum major in his own daily parade—bantering, waving to male fans, blowing kisses to the females. A *Plain Dealer* profile found him both courtly and flamboyantly immodest about his success, an attitude it judged both entirely in character and somehow attractive.

Meteorologist Dick Goddard, who later became a colleague at WJW but was then working at KYW, remembered meeting him while standing on a corner outside the station. Ernie pulled up in a convertible, shouted, "Hey, you're the weather guy!" and then nailed Goddard and passersby with a squirt gun.

Others would imitate Ernie's style, but with less success. John Mahoney, a Channel 8 reporter with leading-man looks and a raffish attitude of his own, "would try everything Ernie could get away with, but couldn't touch him," photographer Ralph Tarsitano said.

Tarsitano remembered one day at Boukair's restaurant, a few doors down Euclid Avenue from Channel 8, where a fountain sat near the door and the Lebanese owner had erected a sort of pictorial shrine to Danny Thomas.

ERNIE GETS A VISIT FROM FANS — DONNA MYERS, 14, (AT TOP), PAT O'REILLY, 15 (RIGHT), PAT MANASTRA, 16 (LOWER LEFT) AND VICKI POULOS, 14 (UPPER LEFT) — AT THE HEIGHT OF GHOULARDIMANIA.

"Ernie says, 'Ralph, grab your hand camera. I got this great idea. I want you to walk in, go past the fountain, and find yourself a nice place in the corner where you can see me come in. When you see me come through the door, start rolling and don't stop.'

"In comes Ernie on crutches, hobbling, and he's got a fake cast on his leg," Tarsitano said. "The whole place stops, and they're looking. Ernie comes by, sees the shrine, puts his hand into the water and makes the sign of the cross. All of a sudden he goes 'Wow!' and throws the crutches up into the air. He kneels down, puts his hand in again, makes the sign of the cross, yells, 'Thank you, Lord, thank you!' and jumps up and runs out. The place is in shock.

"He didn't want it for TV—it was a joke. Just for a joke. But it worked so well he used it on the air. This was Ernie.

"So here comes John Mahoney. 'I'm gonna get in on this,' right? He's got a cape on, and he's hunched over, shuffling like the hunchback of Notre Dame, and he's got somebody in the corner shooting for him.

"Mahoney puts his hand in the water, and the owner comes and throws him out."

Ernie's father used to tell him he was "a fool for luck," and Ernie wasn't above testing it. Claiming not to have an Ohio driver's license, he displayed an out-of-date card from another state and collected traffic tickets like green stamps.

Driving Ernie's Mustang one day, Tarsitano looked in the glove compartment and counted them out: 110 tickets.

"I said, 'Ernie, what if somebody stops you?' He said, 'No one's gonna do anything to me. I'm the King.'"

"Ernie was King," Schodowski said. "He wanted to own the town, and he did. He was enjoying the hell out of being Ghoulardi. Ghoulardi got so big he was missing commercial dates."

One incident stood out, after the Greater Cleveland Safety Council put Ghoulardi's face all over town on bus cards that said, "Don't jay walk! Live longer!"

"One Friday," Schodowski said, "Ernie and I were going to one of his commercial recording sessions in his convertible, and we saw this sign on the side of a bus for the first time. Ernie immediately wanted it for the show that night, so he gave me his pocket knife and drove behind the bus. When it

stopped, he got the driver's attention, and the driver was all excited about talking to the famous Ghoulardi.

"I jumped out and started working on the sign on the other side of the bus. It was really hard to get out of that holder, so we went from light to light. The driver never caught on, because Ernie kept him laughing.

"It took me from East 14th to West 117th and Detroit to get this sign off. Ernie was elated. He lost the commercial gig—I don't know how much he lost because of that—but he had the sign.

"When we got back to the lobby at Channel 8," Schodowski said, "there against the wall, wrapped up and addressed to Ernie, was a sign just like it."

They both collapsed in laughter. Ernie lost a job, and one bus fewer was cruising the city with his image, but he and Schodowski had another funny story.

"Don't jay walk," Ernie said, years later. "That's like telling people, 'Don't fart.'"

At least one of his fans was more impressed with the King than with entertainment's Chairman of the Board, providing a light footnote to one of Cleveland's real-life horror stories.

Donna Adkins, a seven-year-old from the city's West Side, was kidnapped in January 1965, blinded in one eye by her abductor, and then abandoned on the Ohio Turnpike. Once she was safely home, the community that had held its breath raced to aid her and her family with fundraisers and neighborhood collections. Frank Sinatra, whose own son was kidnapped a year earlier, sent her roses.

"Donna would probably have been more impressed if the roses had come from Ghoulardi than from Frank Sinatra," her mother said, laughing.

Ghoulardi paid a personal visit to the girl, bringing flowers and an autographed picture. When her doctor permitted her to watch TV for thirty minutes for the first time, she watched Ghoulardi.

Friends knew Ernie as cantankerous, but they also knew him for his big heart. He was especially benevolent where kids were concerned, and Ghoulardi—for all his image of anarchic irreverence—became one of Northeast Ohio's most reliable fundraisers.

"There's a real kick in knowing that you're helping some worthwhile

Hey, Marshal Dillon!

ERNIE GOT HIS FIRST NATIONAL TV EXPOSURE ON AN EPISODE OF GUNSMOKE IN 1964. ONLY CLEVELAND NOTICED OR CARED, BUT HIS PART COULD HAVE BEEN TAILOR-MADE FOR A GUY WHO SAID HE COULDN'T MEMORIZE MORE THAN THREE LINES OF A SCRIPT . . .

TOP: ERNIE STRUGGLES TO GET INTO COSTUME FOR HIS GUNSMOKE ROLE. AT LEAST HE DIDN'T HAVE TO WEAR A TIE.

BOTTOM: JAMES ARNESS (MARSHAL DILLON), LEFT, AND ERNIE ON THE GUNSMOKE SET.

He had three lines. One was a Ghoulardi trademark—"Over there," but delivered without the familiar "ova dey" inflection—and the other two were about borrowing money: "How about borrowing a dollar off you?" and "How about borrowing five bucks off you, mister?"

The appearance was part of a promotion by CBS, which invited its affiliates to send local station celebrities for walk-on parts in the long-running Western. They were given five lines or fewer, and did not appear in the cast credits.

Ernie's episode was "Blue Heaven," which was filmed in early August 1964 and broadcast as the show's season premiere on September 26, 1964. It featured Tom O'Connor, later a regular on *Peyton Place,* as a wanted—but unfairly framed—killer who risked capture to help a runaway boy find his estranged mother. Kurt Russell played the boy, and Diane Ladd guest-starred as the mother.

Harriet Peters, a TV writer for the *Press*, accompanied Ernie to the set. After a makeup artist said he arrived looking "too aristocratic," Peters reported, fifteen minutes of work turned him into a bum—mussed, unshaven, and dirty, wearing a beat-up cowboy hat, torn vest, faded plaid flannel shirt, and baggy trousers.

Ernie was "serious" on the set, through two days of work in 100-degree heat, Peters wrote, and "his scene had to be shot over and over again because of noisy airplanes. His paycheck will be $299 before taxes, the guild minimum pay."

"The folks at home won't recognize Ghoulardi," he said after looking in a mirror.

When Ernie returned to Cleveland, he was met at the airport by 1,500 fans—plus a band, drill team, and baton twirlers.

cause," Ernie told the *Press*. "This community has been good to me, and now I feel I've got to earn it."

He did most of the earning through the Ghoulardi All-Stars, the amateur softball, basketball, and touch football teams that featured on-camera celebrities and off-camera personnel from WJW. They started as a group getting together after work and on weekends, usually to play teams from other stations. Fans would flock to see Captain Penny tag Ghoulardi out, live and in person, or to see the King nail the Captain at the plate.

As the crowds and their fame grew, however, the All-Stars turned into a major promotional vehicle for WJW and Ghoulardi, and their drawing power only increased as the on-air novelty of Ghoulardi wore off.

The All-Stars were such a draw that the mayor of Eastlake felt the need to issue a public apology when Ernie and other on-air performers failed to appear for a softball game through a scheduling mix-up, and 100 of the 1,000 people who turned out for the benefit asked for refunds.

"It was fascinating to find he was that huge in Cleveland," said Conway, who returned frequently to visit from Hollywood. "He could fill Cleveland Stadium if he wanted to. He did a lot of charity work for Cleveland and kids in the Cleveland area. Whenever he said, 'There's gonna be a baseball game,' or whatever there [was] gonna be, he would fill whatever was there to be filled with people, and raise huge amounts of money for charity."

The best part for Ernie was that it enabled him to raise money for good causes, entertain crowds, promote his show, and hang out with his pals—all at the same time, and all while indulging his passion for sports. When he was passionate about something, whether animals, cars, motorcycles, jazz, or sports, he liked to throw himself into it.

ERNIE APPLAUDS THE ALL-STARS IN 1966, WITH RAY (FRANZ THE TOYMAKER) STAWIARSKI AND, AT LEFT, RON SWEED.

"That's the only way to do things," he said. "You do something—do it!"

He played down the competitive aspect in pregame publicity, once telling a reporter, "We clown around a bit because that's mostly what the crowd expects, but we try to keep the game close." His teammates told a different story, however.

"Ernie was nuts about football, and he was dead serious about the games," Schodowski said.

"We weren't playing against professionals, and I didn't take it so seriously to win the game," Soinski said. "But it meant a lot to him."

GHOULARDI
Chapter 5

"Ernie thought he was kind of a jock," said Goddard, who played on the teams after joining WJW on what Ernie said was an "athletic scholarship"—maybe with a bit of truth. Ralph Tarsitano said Ernie lobbied the station to hire Goddard because he was impressed with his play at third base on KYW's softball team. "He went up to the general manager's office and said, 'We got to get this guy, he's a helluva talent, you ought to hire him,'" Tarsitano said. "But his intent was to get him to play third base for us."

Ernie sometimes pitched in softball, but more often played first base, a position that allowed him also to play to the crowd. In touch football games, he liked to be the field general at quarterback—but only up to a point.

"He was the worst quarterback—he was the worst everything," Schodowski said with a laugh. "And he wanted to win more than he wanted to play quarterback. He had ringers on the team like my brother Paul [an All-Senate quarterback at Cleveland South High School] and he knew exactly when to take himself out and put Paul in to win the game. His timing was incredible. He was wise enough to surround himself with real good players."

DICK GODDARD IN ALL-STAR POSE, 1966.

ERNIE PLAYING BALL WITH THE ALL-STARS. HE TOOK THE GAME VERY SERIOUSLY.

GHOULARDI

The Monster That Devoured Cleveland

The All-Stars played teams from other stations, teams from police and fire departments, company teams, faculty teams, pickup squads representing civic groups, even the Cleveland Browns' off-season basketball team.

"They were picking us up off the ground," Tarsitano said. "Chuck's running around in a circle, going, 'Tarts, we're dead!'" One photo from the game shows Ernie with his leg out to trip receiver and future Hall of Famer Paul Warfield, a scene that would have given Browns coach Blanton Collier nightmares; another shows the mismatch in size between Ernie and massive tackle Jim Kanicki.

Mismatches didn't bother the All-Stars, who kept up a daunting schedule.

"I figure we played about 100 games over the season in all three sports," Ernie told the *Press* in April 1966 while preparing to start the softball season with a benefit for then-new Rainbow Babies and Childrens Hospital. "Figure each game at about six hours with travel time. That's a lot of play and a lot of travel."

Players recall the breakdown as about twelve football games, always played on weekends, and thirty basketball games, played at night on a schedule that could include four exhibitions in a week. The rest were softball games, "and if Ernie could cram in four or five games a week, that was fine with him," Sweed said.

"It was a good time, but it took a lot of time and energy," Soinski said of his single softball season. "I worked a couple nights a week, so my wife didn't care for it and rightfully so—I was hardly home. The next year, I didn't play baseball."

"We played almost every day. I was almost never home," Schodowski said. "He would schedule these games like on a dare. 'Hey, Ghoulardi, you want to play us?' He'd say, yeah. And sometimes he'd forget until the day of the game."

Tarsitano claims one sixty-nine-day stretch included seventy-two games. "We played for the fun of it. We loved baseball, we loved meeting people, and we loved helping people," he said. Team members were unpaid and played on

TOP: GHOULARDI ALL-STARS IN ACTION AGAINST THE CLEVELAND BROWNS. ERNIE TRIES TO TRIP BROWNS GREAT PAUL WARFIELD.

BOTTOM: GHOULARDI ALL-STARS, BASKETBALL TIME.

GHOULARDI
Chapter 5

THE GHOULARDI ALL-STARS HIT THEIR PEAK STYLE WITH THIS UNIFORM.

their own time, though the All-Stars charged a $150 advance per game to cover the costs of their uniforms and travel.

The evolution of their softball uniforms is a chronicle of the team's growth: from white T-shirts with minimal lettering, to blue jerseys with station logos, to pro-style uniforms bearing a stitched Ghoulardi face in 1966. After the first version of the pro uniforms arrived from a major sporting goods supplier, Tarsitano recalled, Ernie dismissed the apparel as "crap" and sent it back; two weeks later, the company sent uniforms that had been made for the New York Mets but returned by that team.

"In '66, we blew out, we were like pros," Tarsitano said. "Ernie decided we were going to win and we were going to look good. 'I'm the King, and you can't allow anyone to beat the King. Right, group?'"

Travel and other arrangements took a turn for the better after Ernie named Tarsitano's father, Mike, as team manager. Tarsitano's nickname was "Tarts," so Mike inevitably became Pops—"Pop Tarts." Professionally, Pops worked as a tool and die maker for General Electric, but Ernie valued him as a friend and sort of advisor who could also serve as spokesman and senior overseer of the All-Stars.

"His life changed," Ralph recalled with a chuckle. "It was really something to have fun like that and have your father involved. He'd be called up to the executive offices at GE, wondering if there was a problem, and the executives were just hoping he could get them autographs for their kids."

Pops screened requests for appearances, waived the fees for good causes that couldn't afford them, promised all charities "we're gonna raise as much money as we can," and booked arrangements. Ernie pronounced it a "masterpiece" when he hired a chartered bus to take players to out-of-town games, making it more of a family affair by making room for wives and even providing babysitting back at WJW.

Crowds of 8,000–10,000 became common. Town and suburban newspapers heralded the games in front-page stories, and elaborate programs were often printed for fans. Once, players recall, Akron police sent an escort to accompany the All-Stars on a trip to the Rubber Bowl. "The Cleveland police said, 'Wait a minute, you're in Cleveland—we escort Ghoulardi. We will take him to the city limits, and you can pick him up,'"

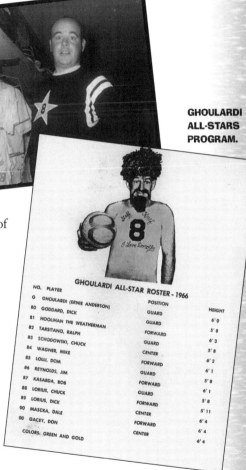

TIM CONWAY IN GHOULARDI ALL-STARS UNIFORM.

GHOULARDI ALL-STARS PROGRAM.

GHOULARDI ALL-STAR ROSTER - 1966

NO.	PLAYER	POSITION	HEIGHT
G	GHOULARDI (ERNIE ANDERSON)		
80	GODDARD, DICK	GUARD	6' 0
81	HOOLIHAN THE WEATHERMAN	GUARD	5' 8
82	TARSITANO, RALPH	FORWARD	6' 3
83	SCHODOWSKI, CHUCK	GUARD	5' 8
84	WAGNER, MIKE	CENTER	6' 2
85	LOLLI, DOM	FORWARD	6' 1
86	REYNOLDS, JIM	GUARD	5' 8
87	KASARDA, BOB	FORWARD	6' 1
88	LORIUS, CHUCK	GUARD	5' 8
89	LORIUS, DICK	FORWARD	5' 11
00	MASCKA, DALE	CENTER	6' 4
00	GACEY, DON	FORWARD	6' 4
	COLORS: GREEN AND GOLD	CENTER	6' 4

ERNIE AT BAT WITH
THE ALL-STARS.

Tarsitano said. "There must have been sixteen cars, lights flying. We never had treatment like this."

Pops also started contributing his homemade wine. It began, Tarsitano said, "when we were playing a football game at a high school. The guys kept saying, 'Pops, these games are getting tough, man, you gotta get some of that Italian wine for halftime.' Next game, he brought a five-gallon jug. Everyone took a swig, and no one could understand why we were so tough in the second half. From that game on, no one could beat us in the second half."

Tough was an understatement, given the experience of Dick Lorius, a cameraman, and his brother Chuck, a director. "One played with a broken arm, the other had a fractured leg, and they never knew until the next day," said Tarsitano.

Pops was even able to turn the tables on Ernie's practical joking. Before one softball game, Tarsitano said, "My dad was trying to figure out how to get to Ernie, so he took a grapefruit, sprayed it white, and actually painted stitching on it. Ernie would put on a little show before the game, warming up the crowd with a microphone—'Hey group, get ready!' My dad went up and said, 'Hey Ernie, how about taking a few swings for the crowd?' 'Great, anything you want, Pops.' So Ralph Gertz threw a couple of pitches, and the grapefruit. Ernie smashed it and pieces went everywhere. He loved it. From that night on, it was one of his routines to warm the crowd up."

"Ernie took that part very seriously," Soinski said. "He was out there to entertain people."

So was Soinski. At football games, he put on the halftime show with his Bob Soinski Parma Garfield Heights Combined Polish Marching Band.

"A lot of times we'd use three majorettes and three band members," he said, laughing at the recollection. "Sometimes we'd increase it for bigger games or

ERNIE WITH BOB
KASARDA AT AN
ALL-STARS GAME.

"Get some of that
Italian wine
for halftime."

GHOULARDI IN ALL-STARS
UNIFORM WITH EXTRA
LETTERING: "STAFF KNIF"
AND "I LOVE DOROTHY."

ALL-STAR LEGACY

The players and crowds remember the laughs, but the Ghoulardi All-Stars were still paying dividends of a different sort thirty years later. Late in 1996, Chuck Schodowski summoned Ralph Tarsitano to the lobby of WJW and asked if he remembered the tall young man standing there.

"I never forget a face, but I didn't remember him," Tarsitano said. "Chuck pulled out a portrait shot of a baby. I said, 'I remember that picture, I took that picture. We were trying to raise money for an operation for this young man.'"

The baby in the photo, now grown, was the stranger in the lobby, holding a picture of the All-Stars.

Tarsitano said, "This young fellow looks down and says, 'Thank you. I'm trying to find everyone in the photograph. I'm alive today because of that, and I really want to thank you.'

"It dawned on me: This is something we did, something where we helped. That's when you feel good. That's what Ernie was all about. I had some tears."

bigger crowds. We might have up to six majorettes, and our wives would join. They would wear white maintenance-shop coats and saddle shoes. The band members wore bowling shirts and white socks.

"Usually one of the band members would play a guitar, which is not exactly a marching band instrument. I'd play this old trumpet that I started off in high school with. I was such a poor player that I was maybe the twenty-second trumpet out of twenty-two. Sometimes my band moderator would say at important games, 'Don't play it, just fake it.' So I used that. We all played different songs, too.

"I put together the band program, and every show was different. We would go under the stands, I would hand out sheets to all the band members, and we would practice formations.

"Ernie would stay out during halftime and announce what was going on, which really helped make it. With six people, we might spell out 'Hi, Brecksville'— we'd just walk around in a scribble, and Ernie'd say, 'There's the *H!* There's the *I!* There's the *B!*'

"We would do things like form a straight line, and he'd say, 'They're making a formation of a pencil!' We'd go back and forth and he'd say 'There's a windshield wiper! It's wiping!' We'd have a line crossing another to make a hammer, and then pound a nail.

"One time we did a sports ball presentation. We started off with a small circle—we were a golf ball. We got a little bigger and we were a baseball. We got bigger and we were a basketball."

But, Soinski added, the King could be capricious with the crowd. "A lot of times, the young kids would want his autograph. Sometimes he gave it, sometimes he didn't. I'd feel sorry for these kids, and sometimes I'd go ask for them. One kid gave me his glove at a softball game, said he was trying to get Ernie's autograph and Ernie wouldn't give it to him. So I went with a pen and the glove and he wrote on it, 'F— you, kid, Ghoulardi.' Real bold, dug it into the glove. I said, 'Ernie! this is a kid's glove!' He said, 'Holy cow, I thought you were putting me on! I thought it was your glove!'

"So I took the pen and changed it. I wrote 'good,' and changed the other thing to an 'L'—'Good luck to you, kid, Ghoulardi'—and gave it back to him."

He could be most accommodating with fans in poorer neighborhoods of the inner city. "Ernie made sure he was in the crowd, and that there wasn't one kid who would leave that he wouldn't give an autograph to," Tarsitano said. "He actually slipped money to kids. I saw it many times."

Schodowski said such appearances confirmed his belief that Ghoulardi enjoyed unusual popularity among black audiences at a time when television's on-air image was almost exclusively white. He thought Ghoulardi's

GHOULARDI

Chapter 5

hipness and fondness for jazz and rhythm and blues contributed to that popularity as much as Ernie's attitude did.

"Ernie saw no color," Tarsitano said. "He always wanted to do something for another person. He always wanted people around him, and he never had a selfish motive on anything he did."

Not that the personal benefit of the All-Stars was lost on Ernie. "To be real honest about it," he told the *Press*, "this hasn't hurt me professionally."

The publicity surrounding appearances helped maintain his profile, and fans at the games were a built-in audience for his show—especially since highlight films of the crowds and action became a regular segment, featuring Ernie's ad-libbed commentary: "There's big Jim Doney—he had a twenty-hitter going before he blew up . . . Look at that cat chase that ball in the outfield . . . Here comes Franz the Toymaker to bat—try to lash one past the pitcher, Franz!"

The popularity of the segments led to an incident that demonstrated how Ernie's famed baiting of management was sometimes in reaction to management's baiting of him.

ERNIE APPEALS A CALL AT AN ALL-STARS' BASKETBALL MATCH-UP.

Program manager Ted Baze "saw that Ernie liked the films, so he said there would be no more shooting of the games, no photographers would be allowed to go out on overtime, this and that," Schodowski said. "Ernie was furious. We played the game, there was no photographer.

"It happened to be on a Thursday. Friday, he came on the air and said, 'I know a lot of you came out and didn't see a photographer. That's because our program manager, Ted Baze, doesn't think much of you viewers. For two or three hours of overtime, he disappointed all of you. But that doesn't occur to him.'

"He just rapped him for what seemed like ten minutes," Schodowski said. "He didn't even tell us he was going to do this, but he had a card. He said, 'If you have anything to say'—and he held it up to the camera—'here's his home phone number.'

"Baze had to get a new phone [line]. It was locked up for days."

The cameras at games were restored.

"Management was really between a rock and a hard place,"

Schodowski said. "The show was so popular they knew they couldn't get rid of him, but they were terrified of what he might do. It was a like chess game, every week. They'd do this, Ernie would counter with that. It was interesting. Never a dull moment."

GHOULARDI
The Monster That
Devoured Cleveland

CHAPTER 6

Parma!

By the end of 1965, the giant tide of Ghoulardimania had receded. Management's warnings and several brushes with disaster had all but ended Ernie's fondness for punctuating his show with firecrackers and explosions.

But he still had one big boom-boom up his sleeve . . .

The three-month run of "Parma Place" became a vehicle for his most pointed comedy, spawned jokes that would long outlive his character, and made him a figure of public controversy once again.

Inevitably, Schodowski was intimately involved. He was the reason that jokes about Parma were first heard on the Ghoulardi show—or heard anywhere, for that matter.

"When Ernie first started the show," he recalled, "I still lived in Cleveland. I was renting, and I was looking to buy a home. I was looking everywhere, and Ernie wanted me to move out to Willoughby, where he lived. Day after day he took me to look at model homes that I could not begin to afford. I said, 'Ernie, we're wasting our time, I can't afford these homes.'

"PARMA PLACE": JANET, JERRY, JOHN.

"About a week later, just before he went on the air, I said, 'I got a home.' He said 'Great, where is it?' I said 'Parma,' and his mouth dropped."

Ernie had lived there.

"When I first came to town, I lived in Parma," Ernie said later. "I just looked in the paper, 'house for rent,' boom, bang, you know, so I said fine. And it's a little postage-stamp place—'Little houses, on the hillside,'" he sang, quoting Pete Seeger's "Little Boxes." "It's just these little lawns."

Schodowski laughed at the recollection.

"He never cut the grass, there were weeds all over," he said. "He was sort of a rural kind of guy, and he didn't like this manicured stuff. He said, 'If it comes up green, it stays.' So he never got along. He just didn't do all that stuff you were supposed to do, and he didn't like Parma.

"When he got a place out in Willoughby, it was an old farmhouse. He had dogs, chickens, a burro, a goat, and he had a bull for a while—a huge bull, you could hardly look over it, and he had this thing chained in a shed. If he just wanted to walk away he could take the shed with him. I said, 'Ernie, why do you have this bull?' He said, 'Isn't he gorgeous, man?' He just looks at it.

"So anyway, I got a home in Parma, and when Ernie goes on the air, he says, 'You won't guess where Big Chuck bought a home—Parma!' I said, 'I got real nice neighbors, a real nice neighborhood, don't get me in trouble. If you keep knocking Parma, they're gonna hate me.'

GHOULARDI

Chapter 6

"This goes on for a couple weeks. He starts saying 'Chuck's been wearing white socks. I hear he's out looking for a pink flamingo and a chrome ball for his lawn.' All around me in Parma are these chrome balls, and I'm saying, 'You gotta knock this off, man.'

"I was the only guy at the station who could do this, because we were good friends. I said, 'If you mention Parma, I'm gonna cut your mike off.' But then I'm thinking that telling him not to do something is telling him to do it—I can't just cut his mike off because we'll have dead air. It's live TV.

"So I got this polka record—'Who Stole the Kishka?'—and I had it cued up. The minute he mentioned Parma, I cut his mike and hit that turntable. 'Boom, boom, bump-bump-bump-bump.' Ernie started dancing—he loved it. So that became the thing."

The bit quickly became a Ghoulardi mainstay. A growing array of pink flamingoes and white socks decorated the set. Every mention of Parma was followed by a disbelieving shout of "Pa-a-arma!?" and a blast of polka music.

"Does this program go to Parma?" Ernie would ask in mock bafflement.

The running gag was more than just a spoof on working-class suburbia, however, as the polka music served to emphasize. Ethnic jokes, especially Polish jokes, were popular in that less politically correct time. They were repeated in workplaces and schoolyards and collected in paperback anthologies.

Parma, with its large population of Eastern European extraction, provided Ernie with a rich lode of material. For much of the community, the city became a lightning rod for jokes about working-class ethnicity, its very name a combination set-up and punchline:

"Parma."

"Pa-a-arma!?!"

"Parma Place" started more innocently—not as an extended ethnic joke, but as a takeoff on *Peyton Place*, the popular prime-time evening soap opera then on ABC. Few shows were riper for parody.

Based on the once-scandalous novel by Grace Metalious and following on the heels of two movies (the 1957 *Peyton Place* and the 1961 *Return to Peyton Place*), the show was set in a small New England town whose Victorian

GHOULARDI
Parma!

propriety masked scandals, dark secrets, and sex that seemed to ooze from every page of script.

A cast list from its five seasons would fill a small phone book. Dorothy Malone was the headliner, but the stars best known to later audiences were Mia Farrow, making her TV debut, and Ryan O'Neal.

Although it had more in common with daytime serials, *Peyton Place* was the first successful prime-time soap. In fact, it was a sensation, especially by the standards of then-struggling ABC. The network launched it in September 1964, ran two episodes a week during its first season, saw it become a top-ten hit, and expanded it to an unheard-of three nights a week in June 1965.

"Somebody said, 'You ought to do something on *Peyton Place*,'" Schodowski said. "Ernie said, 'We're going to do it.' I said, 'What are we going to do?' Ernie said—his famous line—'Don't worry about it.'

"I worried about it constantly. He had no idea where to go with this, and I could not go out and ad-lib like he did. If we were going to do something, I would have to structure some kind of story so I could stick to it.

"But it was really winging it. A lot of it was just throwaway stuff."

The first episode—"Parma Place, Book One, Chapter One"—appeared on Friday, December 17, 1965. It opened with a blast of polka music and a title card displaying the sketch of a nondescript small-town scene, a clear spoof of the opening credits of *Peyton Place*.

Ernie, stepping out of his Ghoulardi costume and character, played John, a "hard worker and good provider" who held two jobs to support his wife, Janet, and their daughter, Susie.

His day job was at Waco Advertising, which was pronounced "Wacko," and was all that viewers needed to know. But Ernie meant it as an inside jibe at a management nemesis, WJW program manager Ted Baze, who came from Waco, Texas. Lest the point be missed, the head of Waco Advertising was named Ted Buzay.

John's moonlighting job, an inspired shot at Cleveland's pollution problems, was working as "muckraker" on Lake Erie.

Instead of living in a boxy bungalow or ranch house, the family occupied a drab apartment that had just enough room for Susie to be offstage practicing the piano—badly—in her eight-year quest to win the Parma International Piano Music Playing Contest.

Almost nothing beyond basic exposition happened in the first episode, which ran just short of five minutes. John came home from a night of muckraking, clad in a dark rain slicker and trainman's cap, and changed into a jacket and tie for his day job while complaining about work and Susie's bad piano playing.

Janet, in white socks and an apron-like jumper, was played by Gina Hallaman, wife of longtime local radio personality Ted Hallaman. She revealed she had just bought Susie a "marked-down" piano, took John's empty lunch bag ("I got a little pickle juice on the corner," he apologized), and handed him his briefcase from the refrigerator—stored there to keep his lunch fresh.

Schodowski appeared as himself in the episode, thanks to a last-minute idea by Ernie that demonstrated how much they were winging it. When the telephone rang near the end of the skit, John picked it up, said, "Who? Schodowski? No, we're here doing a show," and then held out the receiver. Schodowski, wearing a headset connected to a camera, walked into the scene to take the call, dragging a long cord behind him.

"I told you not to call me here," he said. "Let me call you back. We're doing a show right now." He remained on the set for the rest of the skit, ostensibly trying to get off the phone while his headset cord stretched across the screen.

Schodowski's role expanded considerably in subsequent episodes.

Ernie originally wanted him to play every character except John and Janet, as a running joke and a way of saving money. (The performers' union, the American Federation of Television and Radio Artists—AFTRA—insisted that anyone who appeared in sketches join the union and be paid.)

But Schodowski drew the line at playing Susie. Instead, he became "handsome, debonair, downstairs neighbor Jerry Kreegle," which was how John began to greet him, in extravagant soap-opera style. Jerry wore a dark polo shirt with "PARMA" emblazoned across the front in ridiculously large lettering, and slacks short enough to display his white socks.

In a slight twist on Ernie's original idea, Jerry also turned out to be the only on-screen character besides John and Janet—an all-purpose Casanova, buddy, villain, and laborer whose entrances were usually greeted with sudsy organ music.

One plot thread, the clearest takeoff on traditional soap operas, involved Janet's infatuation with Jerry and his apparent eye for her. John's constant

"PARMA PLACE," EPISODE ONE: JANET (GINA HALLAMAN) AND JOHN (ERNIE) TALK WHILE CHUCK SCHODOWSKI ANSWERS A PHONE CALL ON THE SET.

GHOULARDI
Parma!

An Episode of "Parma Place"

"PARMA PLACE": JANET, JERRY AND JOHN SIT ON THE COUCH TO WATCH LAWRENCE WELK ...

... JOHN NOTICES JERRY AND JANET ARE SITTING A LITTLE TOO CLOSE ...

... JOHN ASKS JERRY TO ADJUST THE TV PICTURE ...

... AS JERRY OBLIGES, JOHN SLIDES DOWN THE COUCH NEXT TO JANET ...

... BUT JERRY PULLS UP A CHAIR ON THE OTHER SIDE OF JANET ...

... AFTER JANET BRINGS IN THE CHEEZ WHIZ JERRY HAS BROUGHT FROM THE PARMA GOURMET SHOP, JERRY GETS UP TO ADJUST THE SET ...

... AND SITS DOWN BETWEEN JANET AND JOHN ...

... SO JOHN GETS UP TO ADJUST THE TV SOUND, AND SQUEEZES BETWEEN JOHN AND JANET. AND ON IT GOES ...

need to leave for work provided them with ample opportunity for hanky-panky, and Janet continually spilled beverages on Jerry's pants. Jerry usually needed to leave, a bit clumsily, before anything could happen or she could finish mopping up.

John was mostly oblivious, or too dully complacent to do anything about the romance. But some of the funniest farce in "Parma Place" had John and Jerry both jockeying for position on the couch beside Janet, each one trying to squeeze out the other—sometimes ending with one on either side, an arm draped around her.

A second plotline involved the kidnapping of Susie and the theft of her piano. Jerry was clearly behind both crimes, though John never put together the obvious clues. When a ransom note demanded $8,000, he read it with resignation bordering on indifference. "That's a lotta kapusta!" he said. "There isn't that kind of money in all of Parma."

The need to pay the ransom became John's new reason for working two jobs. And muckraking—which at first seemed to be some sort of anti-pollution pumping—was refined into something like panning for gold or digging for clams.

Standing on an offshore barge, John raked at the lake with a long pole that had a small ladle at its end. "This is it, this is what we're after!" he said, triumphantly dumping a spoonful of "muck" into a bucket. "Notice how nice and firm it is. That weighs a lot, and we get paid by the pound."

JOHN EMPTIES HIS
MUCK RAKE INTO A
BUCKET HELD BY JERRY.

The muck was so valuable, he said, that the crew had to stay constantly on guard against "muck pirates" who would "board our ship, take our muck and then they go back into town and say they dug it—and they take all the dough!

"Kreeg, a lot of guys laugh at a muckraker," he said. "But I wanna tell ya, it takes a lot of talent to be able to get just the right muck and to really pile it up for a night's work. You pay attention to me, and you'll become one of the top muckrakers in this town."

While Ernie enjoyed improvising and had no memory for scripts, Schodowski started writing jokes to flesh out the skits. Typically, Ernie would forget even his punchlines. When Jerry asked John how he got into the business of muckraking, it took three tries before John replied that he had been "a lookout on the Titanic."

"Kreeg, a lot of guys laugh at a muckraker."

GHOULARDI
Parma!

But "Parma Place" drew its real flavor from ethnic, blue-collar suburbia. Punctuated with Polish-American references supplied by Schodowski and Bob Soinski, its observational humor about the banalities and idiosyncrasies of place and character had viewers laughing in recognition.

Where most TV sitcoms used Los Angeles and New York as their primary reference points and looked homogenized, "Parma Place" had the zestier, yeastier quality of homegrown in-jokes. It was the sort of gently mocking material that Clevelanders might expect to hear from the funny guy down at the shop or around the corner, but never on television. "Parma Place" tapped into a vein of humor that network TV had turned away from and would not rediscover until *All in the Family*, and it turned into a bigger sensation locally than *Peyton Place* was nationally.

Like real people, and unlike most TV characters until *Roseanne* and *Married . . . with Children*, John and Janet and Jerry watched a lot of television. The hopelessly square *Lawrence Welk Show* was their favorite— "Our show . . . what a band!"—and bubbles blew from the TV set when they watched it, spastically snapping their fingers and slapping their thighs to the music. John even wrote to the show with polka requests—"Let me know if they play 'Hej Gory Moje Gory.'"

Janet, after the first episode, always dressed in a lumpy bathrobe and had her hair wound up in curlers. She and John never went out, but talked about joining the bowling-shirted in-crowd at the Golden Kishka or Copakielbasa for dining and dancing—maybe to that "new sound," the kielbasanova. Which, of course, sounded exactly like a polka.

ON THE THIRD EPISODE, "PARMA PLACE" CHANGED TO A MORE ETHNIC SCENE.

They made gifts of chernina (Polish duck's-blood soup) and kielbasa (or "kolbassy," depending who was saying it). They dined on "sangwiches" made "wif ongyun"—though Jerry might show up with some Cheez Whiz from the "Parma Gourmet Shop." Jerry's strongest exclamation was "Holy pierogies!" A winter night could be as "cold as a welldigger's wokitch" (elbow), and good reason to "get your gotchies [long underwear] on."

The opening title card of "Parma Place," with its sketch of a small-town scene, was replaced with caricatures of an ethnic man wearing garish high-water pants and carrying a sausage-laden shopping bag, and a round-faced old woman wearing galoshes, an overcoat, and a babushka. "Who Stole the Kishka?" became the theme music.

"After a while, everybody in Parma loved it," Schodowski said. "It really put Parma on the map."

There were dissenters, of course.

"Our city is being ridiculed on TV," Parma resident Ray Guttman told Parma City Council, asking for a resolution censuring the program. "This is a

"Our city is being ridiculed on TV."

—RAY GUTTMAN, PARMA RESIDENT

community we can be proud of. It has good people who support their families and maintain their homes. It shouldn't be subjected to such ridicule."

The weekly *Parma Post* said it was "hard to tell whether the city's new-found image has created more amenity or animosity." Either way, the newspaper said, "Parma is no longer just a suburb, it's now a place all its own."

Soinski admitted to some "mixed emotions" about "Parma Place."

"It was making fun of Parma, and I contributed to it—I would tell Ernie how to pronounce certain Polish words," he said. "I didn't know what a lot of them meant, but I know how to pronounce them." One example was 'Hej Gory Moje Gory,'" the polka that Ernie rendered as "Hey Moura Goura Moura."

"So the way he pronounced them was correct, and a lot of people in Parma thought he was Polish," Soinski said. "It was done as something comical, and a lot of Polish people got a big kick out of it. I think it just got out of hand."

Tim Conway thought it "kind of came to a climax" when the jokes intruded on a performance at Severance Hall, home of the Cleveland Orchestra.

Famed conductor and music director George Szell "said something about the first-chair violinist or somebody being from Parma," Conway said. "The minute he said 'Parma,' the whole audience said 'Parma!?' and started doing this polka.

"Well, it kind of p---ed off the people in Cleveland who weren't in favor of those kinds of outbursts at concerts. They said, OK, stop making fun of Parma. Well, that only heated up Ernie. He did even more, so it became a real conflict. He said, 'If you want me off the air, fine, take me off the air.' Then the influx of mail: 'You can't take him off the air.' It just heated up all the more, and Ernie took advantage of it."

JERRY KREEGLE PLACARD 12/22/65.

The continuing story of Parma Place

THE SETTING IS THE DRAB APARTMENT OF JOHN AND JANET AND SUSIE, SHOWING A COMBINATION KITCHEN/LIVING-ROOM AREA FURNISHED WITH A SMALL ARMLESS COUCH, A LARGE END TABLE, A SMALL COFFEE TABLE, AND A TV. JOHN WEARS HIS DARK MUCKRAKING SLICKER. JANET WEARS A LUMPY WHITE SHORT-SLEEVED BATHROBE WITH A TOWEL IN ONE POCKET, CURLERS IN HER HAIR, WHITE SOCKS, AND FUZZY SLIPPERS. HANDSOME, DEBONAIR DOWNSTAIRS NEIGHBOR JERRY KREEGLE WEARS A DARK POLO SHIRT WITH "PARMA" LETTERED ON THE FRONT, DARK PANTS, AND WHITE SHOES AND SOCKS.

NARRATOR: The continuing story of "Parma Place"—book one, chapter three, page four, paragraph five. (Close-up of a white ashtray with the letter J painted crudely inside, held by Janet) You may remember last week, a package had been delivered to John's wife, Janet. John had discovered that Janet and their downstairs neighbor Jerry Kreegle were suddenly on a first-name basis. (Camera pulls back to show John, in rain slicker, on the phone; Janet is also holding a shirtbox-size package.) As we rejoin "Parma Place," it's moments later as we hear John say:

JOHN: (angrily) OK, Kreegle, you come up and get your ashtray!

(He hangs up. Bad piano music plays in the background)

JANET: Oh, uh, uh, uh, he's coming up to get his ashtray.

JOHN: Kreegle is coming up to pick up his ashtray he left here, and I call him Kreegle!

JANET: Uh, yes, Mister Kreegle.

JOHN: (He places Janet's ashtray on the end table and gestures to the couch) You sit down here. Sit right down here, that's it.

(Brightly) You open your package. Go ahead.

JANET: I can do that after you go, dear. I can do that after you go.

JOHN: (with triumphant insinuation, while walking behind the couch) Just let's see what nice little present you've got there.

JANET: (nervously) Uh, want to see, huh.

JOHN: Probably some little flimsy thing. Let's just open it up and look at the present you've got.

(Seated on the couch, she opens the package and pulls out a long link of sausages, which she hands to John)

JANET: Oh look, a kielbasy! And more! Garlic sausage. (She produces links of smaller sausages) How thoughtful. (She pulls a final wrapped item from the box) Dill pickle.

JOHN: What else is there?

JANET: That seems to be all.

JOHN: Wait a minute, I see something there. (He reaches forcefully into the box)

JANET: John!

JOHN: There's a card. (His voice shifts to smooth announcer tones) Here. A card. "Thinking of you from a secret admirer." (Insinuatingly) I wonder who that could be. (There's a knock on the door; he looks baffled) I wonder who that could be? (He opens the door and seems ready for a confrontation)

JOHN: Yeah? Yeah. Oh. (He steps back, waves goofily, and seems delighted to see JERRY, who steps into the room and pauses to look suavely into the camera for a three-quarter profile "beauty shot." The piano music stops, and organ music swells. There's a cut to Janet, who appears blushingly pleased, demure and gushing)

JOHN: Hello! Mister, uh, Kreegle.

JERRY: Hello, Joe.

JOHN: John.

JERRY: Oh, I'm sorry. John.

JOHN: John.

JOHN: And you know ...

JERRY: Hello, Janet. (He pronounces it Jan-ET)

JANET: Uh, uh ...

JOHN: ... my wife? (Camera pulls back to show all three)

JERRY: I, uh, brought your jar back from the chernina you sent down the other day.

JANET: Oh, that—you ...

JERRY: But I lost that little rubber ring that's in it.

JANET: Oh, oh, think nothing of it. (She takes the empty glass jar and fondles it)

JERRY: I came up to apologize, really, about all the fuss I've been making about the noise. I'm sorry, and, uh, I see you got my present. I sent that up as an apology.

JOHN: Oh, that's perfectly alright, yuh, yuh, big lug, yuh. (He punches Jerry lightly on the shoulder)

JERRY: I got something for you. (He produces white socks from his hip pocket and holds them up, the tops folded over)

JOHN: Oh you. A present for me.

JANET: Oho, look.

JOHN: Look at that, Janet. Mister Kreegle brought me a present.

JANET: White socks!

JOHN: Gee whiz.

JERRY: Are you ready for this?

JOHN: Yeah. (Jerry flips up the top of the socks) Gee whiz. Stripes on the top! Boy oh boy, where'd you get them, Mister Kreegle?

JERRY: I had to drive all the way to the Heights for these.

JOHN: Shaker?

JERRY: Parma.

JOHN: Well boy, they certainly are nice. Gee, thanks, you didn't have to do this. (He takes the socks) Isn't that nice of Mister Kreegle?

JANET: That's awfully thoughtful, Mister Kreegle. (She and John both hold the socks for a moment, then she clutches them to her bosom and fondles them)

JOHN: I'll wear those just Saturday nights only. Boy, those are nice, aren't they?.

JANET: Oh yes, darling, they're very nice.

JERRY: And just don't say anything to Susie about practicing, just let her go ahead, and it sounds beautiful.

JOHN: Oh yeah, she's going to win the Parma International Piano Music Playing Contest, you know.

JANET: We're so glad you like it.

JERRY: How much does that piano weigh?

JANET: Oh?

JOHN: How much does the piano weigh?

JANET: Not terribly much, I don't suppose, a person your size moved it in.

JOHN: A person ...

JERRY: Who was that?

JOHN: Who helped him move it in?

JANET: Susie.

JOHN: Susie! See, it's just a four-thousand dollar piano and heh, as a matter of fact, heh, I know you folks'll excuse me, (he pulls a cap from the slicker and puts it on) I gotta run along 'cause I gotta go out and get the old muck out of Lake Erie. Ha-ha.

JERRY: OK, Joe, we'll see ya.

JOHN: John.

JERRY: Oh. John. I'm sorry.

JOHN: OK, uh, Kreeg, uh, you just, uh, make yourself at home, yuh, yuh, big lug, yuh.

JERRY: OK. See ya, man. (He punches John on the shoulder; John rubs the shoulder)

JOHN: Wokey. (In the doorway, he blows Janet a kiss, shoots a pistol-finger at her, then tentatively steps back in to kiss her lightly on the forehead while glancing sidelong at Jerry, who looks away)

JANET: So, so, so long.

JOHN: (poking his head in the partially closed door) Bye, dear.

JERRY: See ya, Joe.

JANET: Uh, uh.

JOHN: Yee ... uh, well.

JERRY: Yeah.

JOHN: Uh. I'll be home early. (He steps out door, and slams it shut)

JANET: Uh, uh, have a good day. (Janet and Jerry look at each other. He looks at his shoes and digs his toe into the floor shyly, hands folded behind his back. She fusses with her bathrobe, leans over and pulls up her socks, then looks at him)

JERRY: Uh, would you like to sit out on the front steps? It's a nice night out.

JANET: (gushing) Uh, uh. (She crosses the set, puts the socks on the couch, then spots a beverage on the end table and has an idea. As Jerry tries to straighten a ridiculously askew picture on the wall, she walks up behind him with the pot and purposely spills water down the back of his pants—making a little cry of alarm, as though it had been an accident. He turns, and she dabs briefly at his pants with the towel from her bathrobe before pulling back. They look at each other)

JANET: Oh, I'm sorry! Oh.

NARRATOR: Well ... why does Jerry wonder what Susie's new piano weighs? What will develop between Jerry and John's wife, Janet? (Jerry takes the towel from Janet, wipes the spill on the floor and hands it back to her) Tune in next week, as we hear Jerry say:

JERRY: Well, I better be goin'. (He exits and closes the door; she follows and stands against door, looking infatuated)

(END)

Schodowski thought the beginning of the end for "Parma Place" came at a high-school basketball game. Fans of teams playing Parma schools had taken to tossing white socks on the court, and at one game they unfolded a sign saying "Show Us Your White Socks"—a takeoff on the "Show Us Your Lark Pack" cigarette commercials of the mid-1960s.

"The mayor's daughter was a cheerleader and she was horrified," Schodowski said. "She told her father, who was also horrified, and he and a deputation of ladies came down to the station and complained."

The mayor, James W. Day, said "Parma Place" was "a dangerous slur to the community." Councilman James Canaris called the serial "trashy." A group of councilmen met privately to organize what the *Parma Post* called "an all-out campaign against the station" if the show continued.

The opposition was not unanimous. Council President Ron Mottl, Sr., who later became a U. S. congressman, wrote WJW in support of "Parma Place." He and Ernie remained on such good terms, years later, that Ernie taped a radio commercial for the state senate campaign of Mottl's son, and refused any pay for it.

A WAVE CATCHES JOHN IN THE FACE. NOTE THE HIGH-QUALITY SPECIAL EFFECT USED TO CREATE THE WAVE: A HAND-HELD CONTAINER OF WATER, CLEARLY VISIBLE ON CAMERA.

But the protests won out. On March 8, 1966, Bill Barrett reported in the *Press* that "Parma Place" was being "phased out," and "a few more episodes" would appear under a different name. WJW acquired a batch of old Flash Gordon and Buck Rogers movie serials to replace it.

"I didn't fight it," Ernie told Barrett. "I've got nothing against Parma—I used to live there. But there had to be some element of truth in what we presented on 'Parma Place' or it wouldn't have caught on."

"It just wasn't funny to some of the people out here," Mayor Day said. "The school people and the PTA people, particularly, objected. Parma was being made to sound like a foot disease. Students—even students away at college—were taking quite a razzing.

"I'm a great one for a joke, and I believe Ernie Anderson was just having fun. In fact, some people out here think he has helped put Parma on the map. But others thought it just wasn't funny."

"Parma Place" ran for eleven episodes, and not every week. The final installment appeared on March 11, 1966. Set entirely on the muck barge *Boysenberry*, it was a small classic that featured John instructing Jerry in muckraking and both of them getting drenched by waves—or, more accurately, by buckets of water that were visibly thrown by the studio crew. Their off-camera laughter was as loud as that of Ernie and Schodowski, who kept cracking each other up.

"This is the windiest night I ever saw," Ernie-as-John concluded.

All specific references to Parma were deleted, and the title card's ethnic caricatures were replaced with sketches of John and Janet. Ernie's narration called the episode "the continuing story of John and Janet and Susie, her kidnapped piano and bench, and handsome, debonair downstairs neighbor Jerry Kreegle."

But the theme music was still "Who Stole the Kishka?"

Fans of "Parma Place" didn't let the show go quietly. Students at Cuyahoga Community College announced a "Parma Place A-Go-Go," at which guests wearing white socks would get free refreshments. Barrett ran a selection of letters supporting the show, and others appeared elsewhere in the *Press* and in the *Parma Post*.

Kathryn Polo of Parma wondered "what has happened to the American sense of humor." Ghoulardi's movies "may be horrible," she wrote, "but 'Parma Place' puts a little zest in the program."

"I enjoy the program and compliment Mr. Anderson for doing a fine job," wrote Shari Brew, a student at Valley Forge High School in Parma. "My whole Polish family is sure to be by the TV set every Friday night to see the next fun-filled episode."

"It was superb," wrote Mrs. Glenn Fenner of Chagrin Falls. "We admire the Parma residents who felt this sketch put Parma on the map, rather than the ones who protested so vehemently that we will be deprived of this weekly serial."

Wendy Daniels of Cleveland invited Ernie "or anyone else from WJW-TV to visit my neighborhood and write a satire about it. Mr. Anderson has a very creative mind, and it's a shame that a few blue-nosed people can and will put a stop to 'Parma Place'."

The WKYC morning radio team of Harry Martin and Specs Howard, well remembered for their *Congo Curt* comedy serials, said they would work to improve Parma's image. Claiming to be "completely sincere," they said they hoped to stage a big parade as "a mile-long link from Parma to the world," get Parma its own flag, and start a cultural exchange with residents of other suburbs.

"For instance," Howard said, "Gates Mills could introduce polo to Parma."

A month later, the fading strains of "Who Stole the Kishka?" were echoing beyond Northeast Ohio. Ruth Fischer, a staff writer with the Cleveland Play House and a former reporter and editor for the Associated Press, bemoaned the loss of "Parma Place" in an essay for *The Nation*.

"Parma," she wrote, "was the scene recently of a skirmish with television from which the community emerged with a dubious victory. The real winner was the voice of zealous provincialism, and the ultimate loser was the large Cleveland-area TV audience, which, for one brief passing moment, had savored a regional program of rare imagination.

"The point of contention was a lampoon soap opera, sprightly and

GHOULARDI
Parma!

119

amusing but not nearly so comical as the fracas which finally doomed it to oblivion."

Beneath the soap opera, Fischer said, "lurked incisive satire" that poked fun at "middle-class complacency, lake pollution, female glamour gimmicks, bankers, suburban conventions, and—holiest of all sacred cows—at TV itself.

"The consensus seemed to be that the program was provocative but never tasteless," she wrote. "Then, in a sudden burst of civic pride, Parma leaders cried 'Foul!' and demanded that Anderson quit picking on their suburb . . . Overnight, 'Parma Place' became an electronic dodo."

The lingering comic fallout of the show "does not entirely mask the questions raised by the rise and fall of 'Parma Place,'" Fischer concluded.

"Can a community take a long look at its popular image and join in healthy laughter?...

And, more significant, who shall have the power of censorship over a TV show?"
Ernie knew the answer to the final question: Management.

"Parma Place" Is Fun, Debby Says

I have some comments to make on Bill Barrett's article on "Parma Place."

I am from Parma. I don't think that when people say we are Polack that this is an insult because this is helping us get on the map. This is what our mayor was trying to do anyway.

It stated in this article that the school people were upset about it but if so then why did the students go along with it?

I had gone around with a petition to our neighbors, school friends and ... made many

Parma Postscript
The Fans Write In . . .

TV-Radio
Bill Barrett
Parma People Not Pleased
Parma Place Perished

"HOLY PEROGIE, THE PARMA PEOPLE ARE SORE ABOUT PARMA PLACE—SORE ABOUT ITS BEING TAKEN OFF THE AIR, THAT IS!" SO WROTE BILL BARRETT AS A LEAD FOR A CLEVELAND PRESS COLUMN FEATURING THESE LETTERS FROM UNHAPPY GHOULARDI FANS . . .

"Ghoulardi's movies may be horrible (which he himself admits), but Parma Place puts a little zest in the program.

What's wrong with white sox? They are clean, and some people can't wear anything but white sox. What's wrong with kolbassi sandwiches? It's good wholesome food, and we in Parma aren't the only ones who eat them.

And what's wrong with our buying our Cheez Whip at the Parma Gourmet Shop?

What has happened to the American sense of humor?"

—Mrs. Kathryn Polo, Parma

"I notice even Parma Mayor James W. Day put forth his views on the subject. Well, I go to Valley Forge High School with his son, and I get as much razzing from Jim Jr. as anyone.

But I enjoy the program and compliment Mr. Anderson for doing a fine job. And it's not only we teens who like Parma Place. My whole Polish family is sure to be by the TV set every Friday night to see the next fun-filled episode.

I hope WJW-TV will change its mind and leave the program on the air."

—Shari Brew, Parma Heights

"If Parma residents lack a sense of humor (which is obvious), please inform Mr. Anderson that Olmsted Falls would like very much to take Parma's place."

—Mrs. Franklin K. Wood, Olmsted Falls

"What has happened to the people of Parma? Did they ever have a sense of humor? If so, what happened to it?

I realize that munching kolbassi sandwiches at the Golden Kishka is not exactly chic. If the natives of Parma were smart, they'd make it camp."

—Miss Carol Kalcick, Parkview Ave.

"We looked forward to Parma Place each Friday and again on Saturday. From the beginning of the sketch to the final polka it was superb.

I sincerely agree with Ernie Anderson about there being 'some element of truth in it, or it wouldn't have caught on.' We admire the Parma residents who felt this sketch put Parma on the map rather than the ones who protested so vehemently that we will be deprived of this weekly serial."

—Mrs. Glenn Fenner, Chagrin Falls

"I extend an invitation to Mr. Anderson or anyone else at WJW-TV to visit my neighborhood and write a satire about it.

There are 18 adults and nine children (all of school age) on our block, and we could use the recognition.

Mr. Anderson has a very creative mind, and it's a shame that a few blue-nosed people can and will put a stop to Parma Place."

—Wendy Daniels, Eggers Ave.

CHAPTER 7

Killing the Golden Ghoulardi

Anything as hot as Ghoulardimania had to cool off. It did—several times, if you believed the newspapers . . .

**GHOULARDI ON THE
SATURDAY SHOW'S SET.**

In October 1963, only a couple of weeks after *Time* magazine was reporting that Ghoulardi had "caged nearly every teen-age mind in Cleveland," a column by *Plain Dealer* television editor Bert J. Reesing appeared under the headline "Time Running Out on Ghoulardi."

"Some of the tinsel of foolishness has fallen off the ghoulishness," Reesing wrote, making clear he didn't like the fad he compared to the hula hoop. "My eleven-year-old daughter tells me that the kids don't watch Ghoulardi as much as they used to . . . He's been on too often around the supper hour."

He jubilantly backed up the impression a few weeks later, in a long column detailing a "drastic downward slant" in the ratings. "The dubious career of Cleveland's Ghoulardi program at present is going downhill so fast it may spring a sprocket and become unmasked long before Halloween rolls around again," he wrote.

The daytime show was canceled less than a month later, fading quietly in the somber public mood that followed the JFK assassination.

But four months after that, *Plain Dealer* TV columnist Alvin Beam, an admitted fan, delivered a more tempered analysis under the headline "Ghoulardi Still Going Strong."

"The time of the big Ghoulardi fad is over," he wrote. "He grants that he's lost much of his hold on teen-age language. The demand for personal appearances is still there but isn't what it used to be. The mail is down."

Still, Beam thought the quality of the show had actually improved. And Ernie was "more than holding his own in competition with other channels."

The big problem was simply too much of a good thing. The siren of television success calls the unwary to the rocks of overexposure and burnout. Lured by ratings and advertising dollars, WJW set a full-speed collision course for Ghoulardi.

His trademark Friday show, with a big audience of teens and adults ending the workweek, remained an easy first in the ratings. The Saturday show, repeating some material, usually ran a close second to the 6:00 p.m. movie on KYW.

But hints of disaster came with the short-lived afternoon show, *Laurel, Ghoulardi and Hardy*. Running five days a week against KYW's venerable and formidable *Barnaby*, at a time of day when his most loyal fans weren't watching TV, Ghoulardi got clobbered. In total audience, and in every category except teens, Ghoulardi trailed both *Barnaby* and reruns of *Cheyenne* and *Wagon Train* on WEWS. Reesing used the numbers as the foundation of his *Plain Dealer* column on Ghoulardi's decline—though doing so was more than a little misleading, as he compared the weekday ratings from autumn to the sky-high numbers of the Friday-night show in spring.

If its low ratings put a crack in the crown of the self-proclaimed "King," the daytime program tarnished it in other ways. Although the time slot exposed Ghoulardi to a wider new audience, the light of day diminished some of the "underground" quality that appealed to many Friday viewers. So did the different tone of the daytime shows, which were more brightly lit, tamer, and intentionally less intimidating.

Opening Ghoulardimania to younger kids lessened the hip exclusiveness for their older brothers and sisters. Inevitably, for the notoriously fickle teen audience, the novelty was wearing off anyway. They kept watching Ghoulardi, but less rabidly, while other distractions contended for attention.

ERNIE GETS A RIDE IN THE PRESS CLUB PARADE.

Beatlemania arrived in February 1964, propelling pop music past horror movies to the top of teenage consciousness. *Shindig* debuted on ABC the next September, followed by *Hullabaloo* in January on NBC. Months later, Cleveland's easy-listening WDOK-AM changed its call letters to WIXY, adopted a "more-music" rock format, and quickly entered what the radio industry press called an "alley fight" with WHK and WKYC, the former KYW.

Shrieking disc jockeys like "Big Jack" Armstrong, howling disc jockeys like Dick "The Wild Childe" Kemp, and more conventional personalities like "Emperor" Joe Mayer battled with contests and promotional gimmicks for the ears and minds of teen listeners. WKYC's Jerry G became such a teen heart-throb that the station tried to keep his marriage secret; he released a record, got

The novelty was wearing off.

GHOULARDI
Killing the
Golden Ghoulardi

a weekly TV dance show, and engaged listeners with "alligator counting" on Lake Erie and local waterways, a local version of watching submarine races.

At places like Manners restaurants, Ghoulardi giveaways were supplanted by radio station "tenna toppers" and "tenna towers" (for radio antennas), and back-window auto litter boxes.

WEWS, always alert to local programming possibilities, took a crack at Ghoulardi's Saturday afternoon territory in September 1964 with *The Big 5 Show*, a local version of *American Bandstand* hosted by a young announcer from Ontario named Don Webster. Webster had lasted only thirteen weeks against Mike Douglas with a quiz show called *Quick As a Wink*, but *Big 5* became the Next Big Thing for local TV. Soon retitled *Upbeat* and boasting an impressive and eclectic roster of acts, the show became so successful it was syndicated from Cleveland to ninety cities, including New York, Los Angeles, and Chicago.

Stealing a beat from Ghoulardi, WHK disc jockey Kerm Gregory appeared on *Upbeat* one Saturday in a Dracula cape and makeup, singing a parody of "Chains," the 1962 Cookies hit that the Beatles covered later: "Veins/My baby's neck is chock full of veins/And they're just the kind/That I can bite/Oh-oh, these veins of blood/That I can bite."

Local television was changing in other ways. The patchwork of live local programs began to shred and give way to national shows in neat half-hour and hour blocks. The networks, growing in strength, sought more time on local stations, and syndicated shows filled more of the remaining time, as improvements in videotape made them cheaper and easier to distribute.

Syndicated shows also offered consistency, efficiency, and repeatability. They offered sophistication and the steadily improving production values that viewers came to expect, and that stations found difficult or impossible to match on their own.

WEWS gave up and ended *The 1 O'Clock Club* in 1964. *The Mike Douglas Show*, which had sealed that show's doom by soaring into national syndication, moved to Philadelphia with KYW in June 1965, after the Federal Communications Commission ordered NBC to reverse a nine-year-old market swap with Westinghouse. NBC—whose undue pressure on Westinghouse to make the initial trade was cited in the reversal order—reluctantly returned to Cleveland. Channel 3 became WKYC, and Douglas, a favorite Ghoulardi target, became an out-of-towner.

PAUL ANKA, AT THE PIANO, CLEVELAND BAND THE GRASSHOPPERS, AND HOST DON WEBSTER, ON THE BIG 5 SHOW. THE POP-MUSIC SERIES ON WEWS, WHICH BEGAN IN SEPTEMBER 1964, LATER CHANGED ITS NAME TO UPBEAT AND WAS SYNDICATED NATIONALLY FROM 1966 TO 1971.

**GHOULARDI DROPS IN
ON A PUBLICITY PHOTO
SHOOT. DOM LALLI, LEFT,
UNIDENTIFIED WOMAN,
BOB (HOOLIHAN) WELLS,
DICK GODDARD,
CHUCK SCHODOWSKI.**

Within weeks, Linn Sheldon made another target smaller by announcing he wanted to return to adult programming; he cut back *Barnaby* to once on weekends and began hosting a daily talk show, *Three on the Town.*

Newscasts expanded to a half hour. Channel 3's were broadcast in color. So were most of its other programs, as were an increasing number of those on Channel 5 and Channel 8. The first "happy talk" anchor team arrived on WJW with the *City Camera* crew of Doug Adair, Joel Daly, John Fitzgerald, and Hoolihan the Weatherman, soon to be replaced by meteorologist Dick Goddard.

Ghoulardi spoofed them by displaying their pictures adorned with Beatle wigs. Management was upset. News, even happy-talking news, was sacrosanct and not to be mocked. But if Ernie took pleasure in management's irritation, the resolution of the incident must have shown him how deeply he had penetrated the establishment himself: the entire news team appeared with Ghoulardi, wearing Beatle wigs in support of Anderson.

If Ghoulardimania rose and fell like a skyrocket, at its highest and hottest in its first summer of 1963, its fading also recalled Yogi Berra's reported comment about a popular restaurant: "Nobody goes there anymore—it's too crowded."

GHOULARDI
**Killing the
Golden Ghoulardi**

Ghoulardi was no longer novel, simply because he was so famous and familiar. Constant schoolyard repetition of his catchphrases turned some of them into embarrassing and passe cliches. A ten-year-old shouting "Turn blue, you purple knif!" sounded foolish enough to make older fans wary of seeming equally foolish by association.

But other Ghoulardi catchphrases—from "Cool it!" and "Ova dey!" to the reflexive interjection of "Pa-a-arma?!"—remained everyday expressions. The headlines and controversy over "Parma Place" demonstrated that the show could still capture popular imagination and attention like nothing else in town. The Friday audience remained large and loyal, and the Ghoulardi All-Stars were guaranteed to draw a crowd, whatever and wherever they played.

Early in the wave of Ghoulardimania, Ernie had said he could keep the act going for maybe five years. But by 1966, once the boom-booms had been permanently cooled and the furor over "Parma Place" faded, "I don't think it could have been too much longer," Schodowski said.

"If things had been better for Ernie, maybe it would have lasted another year or two. But he was sort of down. His heart wasn't in it."

One problem was the need to keep his show fresh without the help of writers or the sort of production staff that generally keeps talk shows afloat. Schodowski and Soinski, who had other, full-time duties at the station, remained the only regular contributors of material.

"When Ernie was on the air, that's when he had to perform," Soinski said. "He had to be funny right then, had to keep coming up with new material constantly. He was always thinking of new things. He was not just sitting there as a host, introducing recorded bits or talking about upcoming events. He had to keep entertaining all the time. To try to keep that up was very hard."

A bigger problem was Ernie's restlessness.

His wife had filed for divorce after seventeen years in 1964, and the marriage seemed at its end after two reconciliations. Colleagues remembered more than one occasion when Ernie found his clothing strewn in front of the station, maybe with an open suitcase dumped nearby and one of his dogs tied to the front door.

Friends Tim Conway and Jack Riley were beckoning from Hollywood, where they were building careers, and Ernie had the itch to follow.

"Cleveland seemed to be the end of the road," he said, years later. "I looked out there, and there was water."

Conway was going to star in his own series, *Rango,* which debuted on ABC in January. He got parts for Ernie in the first two episodes, as a preacher in the first and an undertaker in the second.

"He can make a living in Hollywood just doing commercials, but he's bugged on getting a steady part in a TV series," Conway told *The Plain Dealer*.

Jack Riley thought Ernie "had a feeling of leaving something that was really great, but wanting to move on. He was ambivalent, I'm sure. It was a big jump for him. He was making a lot of life changes."

"You outgrow being a local hero," Ernie said in a 1975 *Cleveland Magazine* interview. "Don't get me wrong, the kids were really great.

But after a while, I couldn't go anywhere without being stopped on the street."

ERNIE IN ONE OF HIS SPORTS CARS, READY TO CHASE A LONG FLY BALL.

"Ghoulardi wasn't a person and besides, he was dead for a good year before I left town, over and done with," he later told *Ohio Magazine*. "Sure it was marvelous while it lasted. I had a twenty-million-dollar TV station at my disposal and I could do anything I wanted. But man, the adulation . . . was a dreadful pain in the ass. I couldn't go to movies, and I couldn't go to a restaurant. You don't get mad at the people, you get mad at the situation that got out of hand."

By mid-1966, he had already decided "you couldn't be a sixty-year-old Ghoulardi." He described his frame of mind at that time in a radio interview with Tom Snyder in 1989: "I'm getting a little older. I can't keep doing this forever. Why don't I stop now, before it's too late and I can't get a job as a dishwasher in this town, relatively speaking."

In 1987, he told Morrie Zryl, "I still wanted to be a viable performer as Ernie Anderson. I didn't want to end up doing commercials for furniture dressed up as Ghoulardi. Do you know what I'm talking about? There comes a time when it's over—you've done it, you've had your fun, you've had your laughs. We played football, we played softball, we went all over northeastern Ohio and raised millions of dollars. We had a great group of guys. We had a good time, and it was over."

The countdown clock started ticking on August 26, 1966.

GHOULARDI

Killing the Golden Ghoulardi

It was a Friday night, and Ernie joined the crowd at sold-out Cleveland Stadium for its then-annual NFL doubleheader—a preseason exhibition that featured the Washington Redskins against the Minnesota Vikings at 6:30 p.m. and the Baltimore Colts against the Browns in the nightcap.

Running so late that its final score did not make the next morning's papers, the Browns game was tied in the fourth quarter.

"It gets to be 11:00—I used to go on about 11:20—and it gets to 11:15, and I said: I'm sticking this game out," Ernie told Snyder. "Because it's tied, it's the Cleveland Browns, it's football, I was a fan, and I had the kind of show where you could do that—where you could come on after a couple of breaks went by and say, 'I was not here 'cause I was watching a football game. If you think I'm going to come here and miss the football game to open this stupid show, you're crazy.'"

Ernie was summoned to general manager Kenneth Bagwell's office on Monday morning, for a scene he recounted to a number of interviewers over the years.

"He called me in and said, 'We don't think that's very professional and I think we're going to call it quits, you and I. We don't think that's really responsible programming.'

"So I said 'OK,' and I turned around and walked out," Ernie said. "And as I went to the door, and I had my hand on the knob, I said, 'I think you're making a mistake.' He said, 'Oh. What do you mean?' I knew exactly, that I was rehired. And I was. But I realized if he could fire me over that, that he could do it again. And I ain't gonna let him."

Ernie's speech, like the story, seemed to grow in the telling over the years. As he ultimately recalled it:

"I said, 'We have raised millions for northern Ohio in charity football games and softball games and basketball games. I am the best thing this station has at the moment for the community. Maybe not for the air, but for the community. I do more than just show up Friday night. You can't get better PR, and you're going to call all that off?'

"And he said, 'Well, why don't you just shape up?' And I said, 'I don't have to shape up, that's my persona . . .' And he didn't understand that. He had just

"I don't have to shape up."

come up from Atlanta. He never understood me, because his kids didn't understand me. 'Cause they didn't know anybody I'm talking about. I put the mayor down, they don't know who the mayor is. I put Dorothy down, they don't know who Dorothy is. They didn't get it. And he didn't get it because they didn't get it.

"I decided to leave because, after all that time and all that work, that [expletive] hadn't understood a single thing about what I was doing. Why don't I just fold this tent and get outta here before the [expletive] actually fires me."

Twenty-five years later, from retirement in Florida, Bagwell spoke in more conciliatory tones for a *Plain Dealer* interview. "Ernie [was] a very, very talented guy, though he was a pain in the ass to management. And he had that absolutely magnificent voice that God gave him. I don't remember firing him so much as I remember him leaving us."

The Browns lost their late-running exhibition game to the Colts, 24–17, on a night that Ghoulardi was showing a couple of *Thriller* features. The first was *What Beckoning Ghost*; the second, with Boris Karloff, was aptly titled *Premature Burial*.

Three months later, on Monday, November 14, 1966, WJW announced that Ernie had resigned over the weekend.

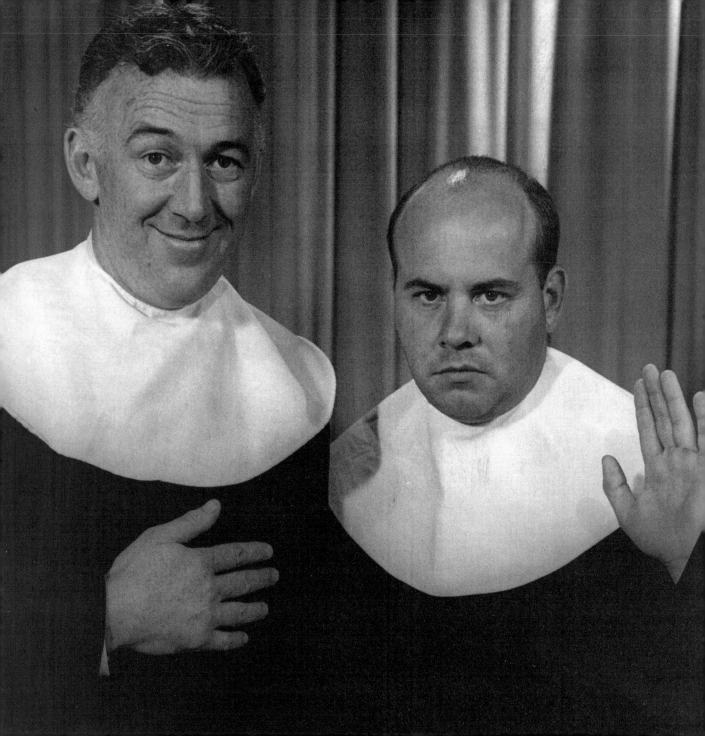

CHAPTER *8*

Ghou-Ghoulardi, Good-bye

One of Ernie's first projects after leaving Cleveland was to team up with Conway again . . .

Ernie did a couple of episodes of Conway's series *Rango*, and they worked as a comedy duo—Ernie as straight man, Tim as the multi-untalented Dag Herferd—on the variety show *Hollywood Palace*. (Conway also appeared once with Joan Crawford in Ernie's role.) Revisiting a few of their old *Ernie's Place* bits, along with material Conway had been writing out West, they also recorded two comedy albums: *are we on?* in 1966, as Ernie was looking past Cleveland; and *Bull!* in 1967.

The albums had their laughs, especially for Northeast Ohioans who'd get the inside joke in an *are we on?* bit called "King Anderson of Parma." The album was recorded at Ohio's Bowling Green State University, Conway's alma mater, and the laughs at the Parma reference were so loud, Conway later had to explain it was not a laugh track. Many of the students in the audience "are from Parma, and all of them are fans of Ghoulardi," he said.

The second album was recorded at the Pat Joyce Tavern, one of Ernie's favorite watering holes in Cleveland, and again it's fun. But a note on the album may have been too close to the mark: "If you found this album distasteful, you will be particularly annoyed by *are we on?*"

The albums "never really went anywhere," Conway said. When the second one came out, there was a mixup that put several thousand copies of a record of whistling inside the *Bull!* sleeve and "nobody ever complained. That's how well it sold," Conway said. "I think it was in the browser bin at the A&P right away."

Still, Ernie and Conway promoted *are we on?*, which at least got heavy airplay on Ed Fisher's morning "Grouch Club" on WJW-AM. One of their publicity stops was the new Friday-night show on Channel 8 in Cleveland. Where Ghoulardi had reigned, co-hosts Chuck Schodowski and Bob Wells—better known as Hoolihan the Weather Man—now held court.

Wells had been the main forecaster at Channel 8, starting there in April 1965, but lost that gig the following year when Dick Goddard decided to return to Cleveland from Philadelphia. (Goddard had gotten his start at KYW in 1961 in Cleveland, then moved east with the station in the reversal of its unusual ownership swap with NBC.)

"They pushed me up to noontime while I waited for something else to happen," Wells told writer Scott Eyman in a *Plain Dealer* profile. After Ernie left, Wells was urged to try out as his replacement—and it made sense for someone who seemed always to be appearing in community shows in Cleveland.

Channel 8 had already tried once to put someone else in Ghoulardi's wig during the 1963 AFTRA strike, but Wells wanted no part of that, telling Eyman "whether you liked [Ernie] or hated him, it was a tremendously big pair of shoes to fill, so I didn't even try." Others did, though.

"They had an open audition," said Schodowski. "I think every deejay in Cleveland auditioned. . . . Quite a few people emulated the circle and the lights and the ghoulish thing." As Wells recalled, "They tested all sorts of people, even rank imitators with the same makeup."

When no successor was found, Wells decided to give the show a try and asked Schodowski to help him with his audition. "My advice to him was, don't try to be Ghoulardi," Schodowski said. He wrote a couple of skits for Wells, and the station decided to put both Wells and Schodowski on the air. Schodowski maintains that he had only wanted to appear in occasional sketches, that he was afraid he would embarrass himself on camera, especially opposite a professional performer like Wells. But the station wanted the duo, and in December 1966 *Hoolihan & Big Chuck* made its debut.

For some fans, late-night TV in Cleveland was never the same. Schodowski said the early weeks were especially tough, when the show was a little stiff and viewers kept comparing what they saw to Ghoulardi's glories. But Hoolihan and Schodowski began to find themselves relatively quickly. Schodowski remembers a breakthrough skit was a parody of the Royal Guardsmen song "Snoopy vs. the Red Baron" with Wells actually flying an airplane while wearing a Snoopy head; it probably dates from early 1967, as the song had cracked the national top forty about a week before *Hoolihan & Big Chuck* went on the air, and held on for about eleven weeks.

As the show worked out the kinks, it can be argued that it had gotten better than its predecessor. Certainly more polished. Not only did the performers in the skits all know their lines, *Hoolihan & Big Chuck* marked the blossoming of Schodowski as a humorist. He was free to develop his own ideas, or to figure out local variations on bits by idols like Steve Allen and Ernie Kovacs. (Schodowski's modesty extends to his crediting, on the air, his inspirations, for example that the Kielbasa Kid came from Kovacs's Kapusta Kid.) Schodowski tended to underplay his contribution. His Hoolihan-era declaration that "my abilities are so limited and Bob has such

ERNIE, LEFT, BOB (HOOLIHAN) WELLS, TIM CONWAY, AND CHUCK SCHODOWSKI AS ERNIE AND TIM PROMOTE THE ARE WE ON? COMEDY ALBUM.

BOB (HOOLIHAN) WELLS, LEFT—IN SNOOPY COSTUME, AND CHUCK SCHODOWSKI IN ONE OF THE FIRST HOOLIHAN & BIG CHUCK FILMED SKITS, BASED ON THE ROYAL GUARDSMEN'S 1966 HIT "SNOOPY VS. THE RED BARON."

GHOULARDI
Ghou-Ghoulardi,
Good-bye

talent for accents and things like that" is typical. Still, Wells said that by 1971 the telecast was "basically Chuck's show." In 1981, a local TV critic called Schodowski "one of the best TV performers in town."

The show rolled on after Wells's departure in 1979 for a Christian TV station in Florida. Local jeweler John Rinaldi, who had watched Ghoulardi in high school and had appeared in some bits on *Hoolihan & Big Chuck*, was elevated to co-host. *Big Chuck and Lil' John*, still on the air as of this writing, is living TV history, a reminder of the days when local TV programming was far more than news and public-affairs shows.

BOB (HOOLIHAN) WELLS, ERNIE, TIM CONWAY, AND CHUCK SCHODOWSKI DURING A VISIT TO HOOLIHAN & BIG CHUCK, 1967.

The sketches hold up as well, and sometimes better, than the surviving bits from the Ghoulardi era. To be sure, Friday night with Wells and Rinaldi was never as openly subversive as it was when Ernie was at the helm, but it still had a capacity for flamboyant outrageousness. The old Polish character played by Schodowski may now be called "a certain ethnic." And Schodowski once said "he could be a Slav, an Italian, any Eastern European, in fact just about anybody." But viewers draw an obvious conclusion about his ethnicity when, say, during "Schodowski at the Bat" he pulls a kielbasa from inside his shirt.

Wells, who became a born-again Christian in 1976 after losing what was by then a weekend weather job at Channel 8, was asked by one reporter how with his beliefs he could justify appearing on *Hoolihan & Big Chuck*. Though he expressed concern about some of the movies, "especially those concerning vampires," he maintained, "I don't believe having fun is anti-Christian."

Fun remained the hallmark of the late-night show. They may not set fire to the studio anymore, but there's certainly a gleeful excess in the likes of Mushmouth, the *Hoolihan & Big Chuck* regular capable of stuffing an entire Whopper sandwich in his mouth. Even Ernie himself became a target of humor; when he and Conway appeared to promote their album, Wells and Schodowski made a gag out of trading Ernie stories on the air, while Conway and Ernie sat, unable to get a word in. Schodowski did not have the anger Ernie brought to the show, but his gentler ways guide a format that has run ten times as long as Ghoulardi did—as well as outpacing more blatant Ghoulardi imitators like the Ghoul and Son of Ghoul.

On the other hand, some fans argue that the polish (not to mention the Polish) applied to the post-Ghoulardi shows did not improve them. To them it was the original seat-of-your-pants, anything-can-happen quality that helped make the show so appealing. Adding to that thinking is the fact that Ghoulardi worked live, the only censorship a post-incident warning of "don't do that again," while these days *Big Chuck and Lil' John* is taped. Still, when the blatant Ghoulardi imitators came along, they would often serve to make the host's lineal descendant, the Big Chuck–hosted shows, look better.

While the Cleveland show was evolving, the burning question for Ernie was, now what?

When Ernie went west, it was with the likelihood of work but nothing guaranteed. The comedy albums had been fun but not successful. He had made serious money in Cleveland, his income up around $60,000 a year when he left, but he had also spent well. A 1965 story noted he "has fairly recently acquired an English sports car, a convertible Mustang, and a gold Honda [motorcycle] that he rides to work"—although, according to Ron Sweed, some of his vehicles were payments from dealers for personal appearances. But what money he did not leave in car dealerships, restaurants, and taverns was up for grabs from the family he was leaving behind, as his first marriage had crumbled.

He often said he went to Hollywood with just a few hundred dollars, and made it sound even worse. "I had a fourteen-pound pair of shoes that you bring in from Cleveland to keep your feet out of the snow," he once told Tom Snyder in an interview. "That was it, pretty much." No surprise then that he and Edwina Gough, the former White Dove mattress commercial star who became his second wife, bunked at first with Ernie's old friend Jack Riley.

"We lived together about two months, until he got a place," said Riley, adding the house wasn't much bigger than a hotel room. "It was my brother Tom, and Ernie, and then Edwina came, and all four of us were living in this little bungalow. [Tim] Conway would come in the morning and—we used to sleep on cushions—you'd have to sit up the cushions so Conway could get in the door. He used to call it 'the ant farm.'"

Ernie had supposedly come out to work on Conway's new series *Rango,* a Western comedy starring Conway as a Texas Ranger, which premiered in January 1967. Conway wrote parts for Ernie in the series, but it was not a success, as was often the case with Conway's series. (Conway once had a license plate that read 13 WKS because, in an era when a minimum of thirteen episodes of a series was ordered, that's about how long his shows lasted.) In 1970 alone, Conway had two failed series, one a sitcom and the other a variety show, with Ernie working as the announcer on the latter.

A *Cleveland Press* story from July 1967 has Ernie working on a low-budget film in San Francisco, as a "lonely, slightly demented convict" who escapes from Alcatraz. Ralph Meyher, a former cameraman in Cleveland then working for ABC, was directing the movie. During production he said, "Anderson is in baggy pants and wanders the street as a kind of scorned and ignored Ancient Mariner type. The camera becomes his eyes as he walks

"Who Is Ernie Anderson?"

through the Haight-Ashbury district and sees the life the hippies are living."

Though Meyher said some three companies were interested in distributing the movie, all the staff and cast were working for free, hoping to get paid if the movie hit. But if the movie was ever completed, it disappeared without notice.

Ernie was seen considerably more on *The Carol Burnett Show* but did not really work on-camera all that often. A running gag in the late '60s had him introduced to the audience as if he were a famous celebrity; although he got paid every time he was introduced, the appearances consisted of a clip of a single appearance played over and over.

The clip replays came courtesy of producer Joe Hamilton, Burnett's husband and Ernie's friend, who was trying to help Ernie's career by getting his name before the audience and masterminding a "Who Is Ernie Anderson?" campaign, complete with bumper stickers. Indeed, when Hamilton and Burnett went to the Tony Awards in 1969, they were often asked, Who was that Ernie Anderson? Hamilton had been planning to let Ernie go on the air, then changed his mind to milk the public curiosity a bit longer.

Ernie was more often heard, as the show's announcer and an off-camera voice in skits; one has Mama (Vicki Lawrence) watching a soap opera, with Ernie as the voice of one of the soap actors—and clearly called "Ernie" by another performer.

Still, as much as Ernie talked about wanting to act, it was not really an option. "He wasn't an actor, he was a personality," said Conway. With an affectionate laugh, Ernie's own son Paul later said he wouldn't cast his father in a movie "if he came back from the dead." (Ernie did appear in a small scene in Paul's movie *Hard Eight* as one of the "pants-on-fire people," but Paul still thought Ernie was a terrible actor.)

That's a pretty harsh assessment, especially when you look at some of

RIGHT: ERNIE OUTSIDE PAT JOYCE LOUNGE, A FAVORITE HANGOUT AND THE PLACE WHERE ERNIE AND TIM CONWAY RECORDED THEIR SECOND COMEDY ALBUM, BULL!

Ernie's silent skits on the Ghoulardi show, where he made use of a mobile, expressive face. And into the 1970s at least, he kept trying to get acting jobs. He once said he did two pilots—one with Jackie Cooper, one with Julie Harris—but nothing came of either.

The reference *Unsold Television Pilots 1955 through 1988* does indeed list Ernie in the cast of a Cooper pilot, *Keep an Eye on Denise*, that was televised on CBS in June 1973. It had Cooper as a former Korean War flier asked to keep an eye on Lynn Frederick, the sister of a British comrade (Richard Dawson), who has come to America; Ernie is listed as a guest star and his role is not identified. There is no listing of a Julie Harris pilot.

A seemingly insurmountable barrier to his acting ambitions was that he could not remember lines, a problem that had plagued him since childhood and was often evident in his Cleveland performances. He appeared a few times on the the 1970–72 sitcom *Arnie*, about a dock foreman (played by Herschel Bernardi) who gets an executive job, but "I had a hard time remembering my lines," he later told *Monsterscene* magazine. "I was so uptight about it that I couldn't do anything. It was a hassle to remember, 'Hello, how are you?' In the movie for Meyher, the director said, "There's not a lot of dialog."

And Ernie tried to run a little con on the director John Badham (or on producer William Sackheim, in one telling of the tale) after he landed a part as a newscaster in the 1974 miniseries *The Law*.

"I said, 'You know what, John, if you really want me to get that myopic look, get me a TelePrompTer,'" Ernie recalled.

"He stared at me for a minute and said, 'You can't remember s---, can you?'

"I did another scene in *The Law* where he said, 'You don't have to remember anything, just know where you're going and ask this guy questions.' And I said, 'OK, I can do that.' But the newscast . . . I read." Similarly, in the 1976 movie *Tunnelvision*, he played a news anchor and reporter and so could read his lines.

Not only was the acting situation rough, the close friendships of Cleveland proved harder to sustain in the sprawling array of strip malls and exclusive housing developments loosely thought of as Hollywood, or Los Angeles. Ernie didn't lack for friends, though. Tim Conway was around a lot.

"We probably saw each other as much as we used to in Cleveland," he said. "We played golf together, we saw each other probably three, four nights a week for dinner."

Riley was there, too, part of what one reporter dubbed "the Cleveland clan, a talented group of TV entertainers who worked together here . . . [and] which takes care of its own." Ann Elder, the Rocky River native who'd been scared by Ernie and Tim back in Cleveland, was another member of the clan, and remained friends with Ernie up to his death. Writer and actor Chuck McCann was another. And Ernie tried unsuccessfully to get other Clevelanders out West, such as Schodowski and Linn Sheldon.

Being from Cleveland was something special. Audiences around the country may have been baffled when Conway showed up on Dean Martin's variety show as the Prince of Parma, or did a newscaster bit on Danny Kaye's series which included references to Jack Riley, Iggie McIntyre (of Pat Joyce Tavern fame), and "our weatherman, Chuck Schodowski." But the folks back home were getting an electronic postcard.

And sometimes the home folks brought Ernie a bit of Cleveland. Ernie loved the wine made by Ralph Tarsitano's father, and on one trip west Schodowski brought him a jug. And not just the jug. After getting on the flight, Chuck changed into his full "certain ethnic" outfit, including the cigar and kielbasa, and came off the plane to greet Ernie in style.

There were newer friends, like Hamilton ("When Carol and Joe divorced," Ernie said, "I inherited Joe"), actor-director Carl Reiner, and Joe Flynn, the Youngstown native who played Captain Binghamton on *McHale's Navy*. According-ing to Schodowski, Flynn, Conway, and Ernie collaborated on a movie script that would provide jobs for all the Cleveland gang.

"Ernie was the governor and Joe Flynn was a prison warden doing some shady things," said Schodowski. Ernie assigns his aide, played by Conway, to go undercover into the prison as an actual convict—only once he's convicted, the governor dies, leaving Conway stuck in prison. Schodowski remembered Ernie saying the movie was going to be made, only Flynn died in 1974 of a heart attack.

Opportunities arose for Cleveland-style mischief. Conway recalled a Monday night, most likely in 1970, when he, Ernie, and McLean Stevenson wanted to see a Rams–Lions game. Because the game had not sold out, it was blacked out on TV, but the remaining seats "you couldn't sit in, because you couldn't see the field," said Conway.

"We couldn't get [good] tickets, so Ernie said, 'Let's go over to wardrobe at CBS.' McLean, Ernie, and myself got three lion outfits and I said, 'OK, we'll tell them that we're the mascots for the Detroit Lions.'" The three of them drove to the Los Angeles Coliseum—in the lion costumes, mind you—and tried to bluff their way past security. "What we didn't know was that they were expecting lions from Safari-Land, down in San Diego, as part of the halftime show," Conway said, so when they arrived, the guard, thinking they were the halftime lions, waved them through to a meeting room with the marching band.

"We're sitting there and the guy says, 'You'll go out at halftime.' And we said, 'Can we go see the game?' And he said, 'No, you're going out at halftime,'" Conway said. "So we said, this stinks, and we went out into the tunnel [to the field]. And [Lions star] Alex Karras looks over at us, and he recognizes Ernie, because he'd seen Ernie on television. . . . And he said, 'When the Lions go out on the field, just go with us.' So on *Monday Night Football*, when they announced the Detroit Lions, we went out.

"Now, the spectators couldn't see over us because these lion heads are so big, so they kept making us lie down on the field. And, obviously, it gets to be about 110 degrees in these outfits, by halftime it's over. We're sweating our a--es off, and we haven't seen any of the game because we're lying on the field for the most part, so we said 'Aw, screw it,' and went home.

"But that was Ernie," Conway concluded. "Ernie never had any qualms. . . . A lot of fun situations came out of the way he was willing, whatever we decided to do, to go do it—right, wrong, or whatever."

Still, Ernie lamented the distance between friends in Hollywood. Conway, living two miles away, was a close neighbor. "Boston's a town," he told writer Bob Dyer in 1993. "Cleveland's a town. There were places everyone went to: Pierre's, the Swamp. It had a center. There's no center here. . . . You get your own campus and that's where you live, and to go over the hill to another campus is a pain."

In spite of all his frustration, though, Ernie was getting rich.

While acting never worked out, he almost immediately began getting voiceover work in commercials, which had been his meal ticket in Cleveland before Ghoulardi hit. Jack Riley hooked Ernie up with Chuck Blore, who did commercial sound production and was "one of the hottest radio guys in L.A.," Riley later said. His approval could get you a lot of commercial work, and Blore definitely approved of Ernie, remarking that Ernie had "an excellent mid-range voice. It gives the impression of warmth and friendliness. It says very subtly, 'You can trust me.' And yet, the distinctive quality of Ernie's voice never intrudes on the message he's delivering."

"Chuck Blore that very day happened to be doing a commercial," Ernie said years later in describing their first meeting late in 1966. "We did some Rheingold commercials, and he told me how to get an agent, because I needed one." Then came the first break, for the Mercury Cougar, "the man's car," as Ernie convincingly declared.

THE GHOUL host of NIGHTMARE MOVIE 61 11 PM SATURDAYS

BUMPER STICKER FOR THE GHOUL.

"I did 'Mercury Cougar . . . the man's car' and went back to Cleveland the next day to videotape some shows," he said, referring to the last few Ghoulardi appearances. "And they called me in Cleveland and said, 'Where are you? You got the Mercury Cougar commercial.'"

The car ad became one of his more famous spots, especially the way he said "at the sign of the cat" (which can still be heard in the "retromercials," or replays of classic ads, on Nick at Nite's "TV Land"). But other work followed and began to crowd out even the attempts at acting jobs. And the biggest break in his announcing career was still around the corner.

Meanwhile, back in Cleveland, where Hoolihan and Big Chuck tooled along as the lineal descendants of Ghoulardi, another personality was about to try re-creating the spirit of the show.

This was Bowling Green State University senior Ron Sweed, Ernie's one-time gofer, who had decided to step in front of the camera as a character he called "The Ghoul.". No question, the Ghoul was derived from Ghoulardi; Sweed had asked Ernie's permission before portraying the character, who looked like Ghoulardi, and borrowing catchphrases. Sweed had his own Camera Fo' as well as his own "Parma Place," called "Spencer and Mongolia" (after the first names of a couple named the Ghoulouskis). He would have taken the Ghoulardi name as well, only Storer Broadcasting, Channel 8's owner, claimed to own it and had already won a court fight over it.

Making his debut in February 1971, on WKBF (Channel 61), an independent station owned by Kaiser Broadcasting, the Ghoul was added to Kaiser's Detroit station WKBD in 1972, and from 1973 to 1975 was on all the Kaiser stations, including those in Boston, Philadelphia, and San Francisco. The Ghoul accordingly reached a vaster audience than Ghoulardi had, although Sweed has acknowledged he was not as inventive as Ernie had been.

Playing to an anarchic audience of teens and twentysomething men, the Ghoul was more interested in blowing up objects (though never, contrary to myth, live animals) than sneaking in a hip joke. One of his most famous bits involved Froggy the Gremlin, a character first seen on the children's shows *Smilin' Ed's Gang* (hosted by Smilin' Ed McConnell from 1950 to 1955) and *Andy's Gang* (hosted by Andy Devine, after McConnell died, from 1955 to 1960). According to horror-host historian Elena Watson, the Ghoul would blow up Froggy as often as three times per show. To this day, though, some

THE GHOUL, IN A
HOLIDAY MOOD.

fans mix up memories of the Ghoul with memories of Ghoulardi—for example, assuming a song from the latter was actually played by the former—because of their similarities.

Sweed temporarily lost his Cleveland perch in 1975 when Channel 61 went out of business. Sweed and Kaiser battled over who owned the Ghoul, but in 1976 he was back on the air, in costume, on WXON in Detroit and, after Channel 61 went back on the air, in Cleveland. By the late '90s, he was off Cleveland TV again but still remembered as a personality, appearing at local clubs, on radio, and in occasional TV specials in Detroit.

The Ghoulardi lineage took a weird turn in 1987 after Canton TV station WOAC (Channel 67) began carrying the "Son of Ghoul," a character played by musician and film editor Kevin Scarpino. At times Scarpino has associated himself with both Ghoulardi and the Ghoul; in a 1993 interview with the *Akron Beacon Journal*, he said, "I'm keeping the Ghoulardi tradition alive" and that he had once won a Ghoul look-alike contest after which Sweed called him Son of Ghoul.

Scarpino officially followed WOAC's "Cool Ghoul," played by George Cavender; he had worked on Cavender's crew and was costumed differently from Ghoulardi and the Ghoul. But Sweed thought the Son's act too close to Ghoulardi's and the Ghoul's—even phrases like "turn blue" had been appropriated—and Scarpino, in Sweed's view, did not have permission.

Sweed sued. In 1989 , a Stark County Common Pleas Court judge ruled that all horror-movie hosts look alike: "Horror-show hosts can be categorized as being offbeat characters, hosting old movies, performing comic skits, and appealing to the preteen age to mid-twenties age group." Scarpino continued to play Son of Ghoul, on WOAC until 1996 and then on WAX and WAOH, a tandem of low-power stations in Cleveland and Akron. Still, the remaining members of the Ghoulardi inner circle treat him as something of an interloper.

As people back in Cleveland lined up to be Ghoulardi's heir,

Ernie was enjoying the greatest success of his life and a seven-figure income.

ABC, long third among the three major networks, was laying the groundwork for a ratings explosion that would find it at the top of the heap by the mid-1970s. Though the key component of the plan was finding series that would reach out to children and young adult viewers, another component, now commonplace, was a customized approach to promoting its shows. ABC began promising new glories in each night's individual episodes instead of generalized pleas to watch a whole series.

Wanting a distinctive voice to add urgency, excitement, or humor to the ads, ABC turned to an increasingly familiar name. "I went down and did a recording, which they put to film for ABC Sports," Ernie said. "Then I did more ABC stuff to film." That put him in position to be the voice in the customized spots, in effect the voice of the entire network.

The first announcement he remembered doing was for *That's My Mama*, a 1974–75 situation comedy about a young barber and his mother. His promotion of *The Love Boat,* which began as a series in 1977, proved among his most memorable, as was the way he'd say, "Tonight . . . on a very special (your show's name here) . . ." Millions of viewers' first impression of *Roots* and *The Winds of War* came from Ernie's reading of the titles.

So successful were his efforts for ABC, he was also signed by ABC stations around the country to do their promotional spots, as well as becoming the voice of individual shows such as *America's Funniest Home Videos.*

"His real achievement in this business was his ability as an announcer and a cold reader," said Linn Sheldon, and Ernie commanded top dollar. (CBS, he once said, made a deal with him, only to renegotiate it once they realized what Ernie cost.) "I went into ABC with him once, and I had just started smoking a cigarette," said Sheldon. "He read about four spots, sight unseen, and made about $30,000, and we were out of there before I finished the cigarette."

Voice work was also a perfect job for Ernie's lifestyle. As he so often said, he didn't have to dress up, he didn't have to wait around a TV studio or a movie set. On the sets, he said, "You've got to stand around with makeup, you know, Kleenex on your collar so it doesn't get on your shirt, and you hear the same joke the grip told at six o'clock in the morning again at three o'clock in the afternoon. And you're there all day and you're doing it over and over and over again. . . . I hated it."

Better yet, in voice work the lines were written down right in front of him. And he recognized the value of the business enough to take some care of his voice, saying, for example, that he stayed away from doing voices in cartoon series because "it's voodoo on your throat, it really is. If you listen, those folks really scream."

The voice success was the final blow to his acting career. "The more he did the voiceovers, the less time he had for television," said Tim Conway. "As a matter of fact, when Carol Burnett wanted to use him in some guest spots on *The Carol Burnett Show*, he couldn't take them because he was so jammed

King Anderson of Parma

AFTER ERNIE LEFT CLEVELAND, HE AND TIM CONWAY TEAMED FOR TWO COMEDY ALBUMS, ARE WE ON? AND BULL! ALTHOUGH THE ROUTINES FEATURED DAG HERFERD, THE CHARACTER CONWAY HAD PLAYED ON THE OLD ERNIE'S PLACE SHOW ON CHANNEL 8, CONWAY SAYS HE WROTE MOST OF THE BITS LATER FOR HIS APPEARANCES WITH STEVE ALLEN AND ON OTHER TV SHOWS. STILL, ONE BIT FROM ARE WE ON? PLAYED ESPECIALLY WELL WITH THE NORTHEAST OHIOANS IN THE AUDIENCE IN BOWLING GREEN, OHIO, WHERE THE ALBUM WAS TAPED.

Ernie: If we could find a way to ensure peace throughout the world and abolish the threat of war, well, there is a small country that has found this secret of peace. It's the small European country of Parma.

Tonight we are going to talk to the man who governs this peaceful nation, Mr. Dag Herferd. Hello, Mr. Herferd.

Conway: Tunic.

Ernie: What does that mean--"hello" in your country?

Conway: No, that means "tunic." You're standing on my tunic.

Ernie: I'm sorry, Mr. Herferd.

Conway: Quite all right.

Ernie: Now, I understand you are King Anderson's brother. In other words, you're really a prince.

Conway: Well, thank you. You're not bad yourself.

Ernie: Mr. Herferd, in the last 300 years there have been many major conflicts in the world. Now, how do you account for the fact that Parma was not engaged in any of these wars?

Conway: Well, nobody asked us. A lot of guys just sat around and read magazines.

Ernie: Do you have an army?

Conway: Yes, we do. As a matter of fact, we have a very effective army. We have 3,000 women in the army--they're all privates--and we have eleven men.

Ernie: Three thousand women are privates? What are the men?

Conway: Uh, they're pretty happy. A lot of them spend their leave time right in the barracks. 'Cause we have lights-out early.

Ernie: Do you have an air force?

Conway: Yes, we do. We have a Royal Parma Air Force. We have 300 members of the Royal

Parma Air Force.

Ernie: I was told you didn't have any planes in Parma.

Conway: Well, we don't. But don't tell the cadets. They've already rented a hall for the spring formal. . . .

Ernie: How do you teach them to fly if you don't have any airplanes?

Conway: Well, we have a tower. It's about a hundred feet high. And we send all the cadets up on this tower and we strap wings to their arms and then they jump off the tower.

Ernie: Well, where do they land?

Conway: In a big pile down at the bottom.

Ernie: What in the world does that teach them?

Conway: Well, it teaches them not to jump off that tower. Kinda stupid.

Ernie: Do you have a navy?

Conway: No, but we have eight soldiers that can float. They can swim if they have to--bayonets in their teeth--going right in.

Ernie: What kind of weapons do you have?

Conway: Here's our most effective weapon. Perhaps you'd like to see this. This is what we call our gun.

Ernie: That looks like a plain rock to me. How does it work?

Conway: What you do is, when you see the enemy coming, you take this gun and throw it at him and you yell "bang!" It's quite effective. We're working on a new one now--it's the same thing only with a silencer.

Ernie: How does that new one work?

Conway: It works the same way only you don't yell "bang!" You just yell "snarf!"

Ernie: Thank you for visiting with us, Mr. Herferd. And before you go, would you have a message for the other countries of the world, something that might help them live in peace, as your country has done. . . .

Conway: As a matter of fact, we have a little folk song we sing here in Parma that has helped to hold peace here in our little country. If you wouldn't mind, I could sing it for you.

Ernie: Sure, go ahead.

Conway: It goes something like this:

"Hmmmmm. Man has fought to protect his home.

Man has fought to protect his women.

Hmmmm.

Man has fought to protect his country and his rights.

Fighting, fighting, fighting, fighting.

To have less fighting in the world, we've got to stop fighting so much."

Ernie: Well, that stinks.

ERNIE AND TIM CONWAY RECORDING TRACKS FOR ARE WE ON? AT BOWLING GREEN STATE UNIVERSITY.

with doing these voiceovers.... Once in a while he'd come down and do a part on Carol's show, but for the most part he was so inundated with the voiceover spots, he just had no time for that anymore."

He did make other tries and had a billed role, as a news anchor and reporter in the semi-underground movie *Tunnelvision* in 1976. It was a set of comedy skits supposedly parodying television (with Ernie also serving as the voice of the fictional Tunnelvision network). The movie is of special interest to Northeast Ohioans because Edwina Anderson appears in it, too, as a co-host of one show with Quant O'Neil, Ernie's character. But *Tunnelvision* is deeply awful, despite a cast including Chevy Chase, Howard Hesseman, Ron Silver, Laraine Newman, John Candy, Betty Thomas, and Al Franken. *The Motion Picture Guide* reasonably gave the movie no stars and called it "ugly and highly unfunny.... this complete waste of time."

ERNIE AS A NEWS ANCHOR AND EDWINA GOUGH ANDERSON, CO-ANCHOR, IN THE MOVIE TUNNELVISION.

Still, Ernie was rich, successful, and somewhat famous, as Northeast Ohio writers would periodically remind folks on their way to retelling Ghoulardi stories. "To this day," he said in 1993, "someone from Chattanooga will call and do a phone interview and say . . . 'Just say "The Lu-u-uhv Boat."'"

"We used to have great parties and stuff," said Jack Riley. "His seventieth birthday party was great. Also his sixty-fifth. I remember a great band there. Jack Sheldon . . . [a] great trumpet player. He was a friend of Ernie's. . . . Ernie was a big jazz fan. In the last part of his life that was his big thing. Every Tuesday night he'd go to a place called the Moonlight Tango Cafe in Studio City. He loved big bands."

"It was fun," said Tim Conway. "It was truly fun. We owned places in Maui. He had the place next door, and we would come over with all the kids. Be over there for maybe a month at a time." Ernie also traveled overseas, to New York, and to Boston, near where he grew up—one of his favorite cities.

Still, his final years had their down side. His second marriage ended. (There would be a third Mrs. Anderson, Bonnie, and Riley for one thinks "they were truly in love." Sadly, she would die five days after Ernie.) He had a stroke in 1995, which made it difficult for him to walk and impaired his memory. He did not work at all in 1996, when cancer began in his lungs, although he continued to be heard on *America's Funniest Home Videos,* where producer Vin DiBona reused old Ernie announcements. To visit his favorite nightspot, Riley said, "they'd drive up to the front and actually carry him into the place." And even before illness ravaged him, Ernie's moment as an announcer may have begun to pass, as what had been fresh twenty years ago began to sound "too announcery," in Ernie's phrase, to other people.

Cleveland had always continued to love Ernie, and even old enemies mellowed. When he came back to host the local Emmys in 1981, *Cleveland Press* critic Bill Barrett, who had been especially vocal against Ghoulardi, said Ernie was nervous about failing in front of his old friends but said "it's not likely to happen" and Ernie was an "old pro." Ernie also received the Cleveland Association of Broadcasters' award for contributions to Cleveland broadcasting in 1996. (He was too ill to attend in person but videotaped a thank-you.)

In a 1987 radio interview, Ernie said, "Even today I walk down the streets of Los Angeles and perfect strangers will point to me and go, 'Ghoulardi.'"

There was national notice of Ernie, too, including an appearance on cult-movie host Joe Bob Briggs's show in 1991 (which proved to be the last time Ernie donned Ghoulardi gear on the air) and visits to Tom Snyder's radio show and David Letterman's TV series. (The latter did not go well, Ernie later said, because he wanted to banter and Letterman was not interested.)

Still, over the years Ernie's interviews had their cranky, if not bitter, moments.

In a 1988 chat with Schodowski and Rinaldi, he said he liked working because he could tell his wife, "I'd like to stay here, dear, and let you rag on me, dear, but I've gotta go to work." There was an obvious edge to the supposed joke. His comments about Cleveland could be nasty—as when he told *Ohio Magazine* "Cleveland is a dreadful place, full of petty, narrow, little people"—but Schodowski thinks Ernie did not mean them.

He even turned on himself in his final TV interview, saying that he could have been another Howard Stern, but he didn't have the nerve to go that far. In fact, broadcast standards in the 1960s would never have let him go as far as Stern has. "I think he would have been restrained so much, you wouldn't have seen the real Ernie," Conway said.

In that final interview, with TV reporter Mike Olszewski in 1996, Ernie looked ill, struggled to remember things, and spoke intemperately of old friend Tim Conway and protégé Ron Sweed, even as the videotape rolled. But Olszewski sensed that Ernie knew his end was near, telling the reporter "you're going to need that [interview] tape when I die."

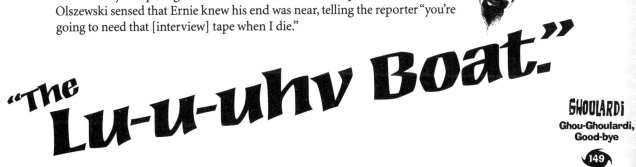

"The Lu-u-uhv Boat."

GHOULARDI
Ghou-Ghoulardi,
Good-bye

149

"who wrote this crap?"

Conway himself remembers not seeing Ernie much in his final months, but mainly because Ernie did not ask to get together when they talked on the phone. "I knew in a sense he didn't want me to. Had I been in the same situation, I wouldn't have wanted him to see me.

"I think we enjoyed so much together in different times, it was painful for him to know that those weren't going to occur again," said Conway. "As time went on, he got worse. The last time I saw him was in a wheelchair, really immobile. His memory was fading. He still had the Ernie kick . . . but it was beating him. And he didn't want to be seen defeated."

Riley, though, kept stopping by, was there for Ernie's last TV interview, and saw Ernie just days before his death. "He was still feisty," said Riley. "Basically he was the same personality, which was great. I'd choose that over being able to move but [having] no brain. . . . I was surprised when he died. I thought he was doing well that weekend." Still, on February 6, 1997, Ernie was gone.

There were front-page obituaries in *The Plain Dealer* and the *Akron Beacon Journal*, a tribute special on *Big Chuck and Lil' John*, radio reminiscences, and memorials on *America's Funniest Home Videos* and *The Drew Carey Show*.

Always the sad emotions came with a story: Ernie and his motorcycle, say, or Ghoulardi setting fire to a studio. And when hundreds of friends, many of them part of the "Cleveland clan," gathered at Forest Lawn Memorial Park in Hollywood Hills to give Ernie his last farewell on February 11, the laughs came as fast as the tears.

"He wouldn't want any of us to be unhappy," said Rita Vennari, Ernie's commercial agent. "We're trying." And Ernie's second wife, Edwina, had said before the service, "We're going to keep it the way he would have done it, upbeat and irreverent—though we will clean up the language a little bit."

Flanking the casket were two pictures: one a professional drawing of Ernie, the other a color photo of him in a bright red dress, white string of pearls, and black feathered cap. Some of the mourners wore Ghoulardi T-shirts. After the minister read selections from scripture, Jack Riley began his remarks by complaining that the minister had stolen his selections.

"Ernie probably has his picture next to several words in the dictionary. Feisty, irreverent, irascible are the main three," Riley said. "Some said Ernie was cranky, self-inflated, and a blowhard—and that was just his family. . . .

When Ernie was working, he said only three things in a session: 'Hello.' 'You call these earphones?' And, 'Who wrote this crap?'"

Conway, who flew in from Paris for the service, took people back to the Cleveland days. He remembered Ernie's vulgar greeting in their first meeting, and gave another encounter new resonance.

"Ernie and I were sitting in a bar called the Swamp," he said. "An awful place . . . We were at the bar having a couple of drinks and this guy comes in and says, 'Did you hear? One of the news announcers just died of a heart attack.' We were both shocked. Ernie replied, 'That's terrible,' paused for a moment, then said, 'Gimme an egg and a beer.' And this phrase became Ernie's way of just getting on with life." And Conway carried on, too, saying, "An egg and a beer, Ernie."

After Ernie's service, about 300 people gathered at the Moonlight Tango Cafe, Ernie's old hangout, and listened to a tape called "Mr. Warmth," a collection of Ernie's more outrageous audio outtakes. Through both events, Ernie was still doing what he'd always loved to do: make people laugh.

Bob Ridgley, another announcer and friend of Ernie's, had died two days after Ernie, and Riley imagined Ridgley arriving at heaven and asking if Ernie was there. "The angel at the gate answers 'No,'" said Riley. "Ridgley tells the angel, 'Good, because I want to be the voice of heaven.' He goes walking around heaven and suddenly hears, from one of the rooms, a booming voice saying, 'The Lu-u-uhv Boat.' Ridgley says, 'Hey, what's that? I thought you said Ernie Anderson wasn't here.'

"The angel says, 'He's not. That's God. He just thinks he's Ernie Anderson.'"

TV icon 'Ghoulardi' dies at 73

GHOULARDI

Ghou-Ghoulardi, Good-bye

151

The Ghoulardi Legacy

June 1997. In the Highland section of Akron, a shoe-repair shop had an odd display in its window: a chair with a picture of Ghoulardi sitting on it . . .

RIGHT-HAND PAGE:

TOP LEFT:
"BIG CHUCK"
SCHODOWSKI, IN SWEAT-
SHIRT IMPRINTED WITH
THE OFFICIAL GHOULARDI
LOGO AND ERNIE'S H-LESS
"GOULARDI" SIGNATURE.

TOP RIGHT:
BOB SOINSKI IN THE
CONTROL ROOM AT
WJW-TV, 1997.

BOTTOM LEFT:
RALPH TARSITANO, WJW
NEWS VIDEOGRAPHER
AND MAINSTAY OF THE
GHOULARDI ALL-STARS.

BOTTOM RIGHT:
RON SWEED AND HIS
GHOULISH ALTER EGO,
AS THEY APPEAR TODAY.

Bob Ferguson, who operates the shoe shop, is one of those who mourned the passing of Ernie Anderson but keeps the memory of Ghoulardi alive. (His window displays are known for their skewed humor—when people told him he should have a bunny for Easter, he put up a mannequin dressed as a Playboy bunny.) The walls of his shop bear images of Ghoulardi.

Over in Kent, you could walk into a used-record shop and find a copy of a Duane Eddy single, in a picture sleeve, displayed prominently on the wall. A handwritten sticker notes that the record's B side is the "Ghoulardi theme" ("Desert Rat"). In that same store, you would hear discussions about which songs Ghoulardi used on the air. When told a customer was about to interview Chuck Schodowski, the store operator immediately asked, "Find out which version of 'Cherokee' they used on the show."

The memory of Ghoulardi not only lives on more than thirty years after the character stopped appearing regularly on TV, it has outlasted the man who played the part. A brisk business in Ghoulardi-emblazoned apparel continues. Ron Sweed, known both as the Ghoul and for his work for Ghoulardi, is back on the radio, hosting a weekend show on WNCX-FM. People are e-mailing a Cleveland Web site to find out how to get Ghoulardi shirts. An oldies station, WMJI-FM, still does occasional Ghoulardi tributes featuring music from the old show and memories from Sweed, Schodowski, and the fans who call in to share the moment.

The last picture Clevelanders had of Ghoulardi was a bleak one, of a hairless, red-eyed Ernie interviewed by TV reporter Mike Olszewski while struggling against illness and age and the results of a lot of hard living. But the memory that endures is more of a fearless, bearded wild man joking his way through close to 200 Friday nights.

Comic actor Drew Carey invoked the flamboyant Ernie for the nation as the former Clevelander wore a faded Ghoulardi sweatshirt on his ABC sitcom. Carey went even further, dedicating an episode of *The Drew Carey Show* to Ernie's memory. Viewers outside Northeast Ohio may have been puzzled at the mention of Ghoulardi—one Web site devoted to Carey lists "Who is Ghoulardi?" among its frequently asked questions—but the folks back home understood. Carey's show in some respects continues a tradition of Ghoulardi humor, at once derisive, self-deprecating, and somehow affectionate.

Carey noted how important Ghoulardi had been when he was growing up in Old Brooklyn. He even signed up with Ernie's commercial agency when he hit Hollywood—although he never got a chance to meet Ernie.

"It was Ghoulardi when I was in grade school and the Ghoul when I was in high school," said Carey. "Everyone was telling Parma jokes all the time.

GHOULARDI
Epilogue

Parma was a city we made fun of while everybody made fun of us." Parma references show up on Carey's show, for which the original theme song was the comic ode "Moon over Parma."

Carey and producer Bruce Helford first heard a band play that ditty about love on the North Coast in South Euclid's House of Swing in 1995. But the song was also part of the Ghoulardi legacy, since composer Bob "Mad Dog" McGuire had originally written it for Chuck Schodowski in 1973.

Carey is not the only performer keeping Ghoulardi's memory alive. As this book was being written, the Cramps were back in a studio, presumably to reclaim the title *Trouser Press* has given them of "punk's greatest living rockabilly zombies." The Cleveland music Web site, created by John Petkovic, sums up the Cramps as a "psychobilly, trash-horror band," but no matter what they're called, their Ghoulardi roots show constantly.

Stow High School graduate Erick Purkhiser conceived the band the Cramps "while watching B-movies on late-night area TV," and *Trouser Press* adds the grace note, calling Purkhiser—who performed under the name Lux Interior—"clearly a student of Cleveland television's Ghoulardi." Their recordings occasionally sound as if they've been lifted off Schodowski's turntable, their titles like some '90s high-kitsch variant on Ghoulardi movies: "The Creature from the Black Leather Lagoon," "Journey to the Center of a Girl," "Rock on the Moon." Ghoulardi was hardly the only influence on the Cramps—who've also recorded "Mad Daddy," an ode to the late deejay Pete Myers—but he's a pervasive one. They named an album *Stay Sick!* and one night in Los Angeles Lux hosted a radio show under the name the Purple Knif.

Airplay on "Ghoulardi" gave a boost to local bands, such as Tom King and the Starfires (the "Stronger Than Dirt" combo who evolved into the Outsiders) and the Baskerville Hounds ("Space Rock, Parts 1 and 2"). But the Cramps are one of many indications of how the influence spread.

On their 1992 post-breakup album *The Splendor of Sorrow*, the Easter Monkeys—with guitarist Jim Jones, formerly of Cleveland's Pere Ubu and the Mirrors—included a song called "Camera Fo'." The Ghoulardi tribute had the recurring lines "Stay sick! Turn blue! Ghoulardi's been waitin' up for you," and was followed by the Ghoulardi-esque "My Baby Digs Graves."

Both the East and West coasts boasted separate bands known as the Purple Knifs. Actually the West Coast version was called Orbit and the Purple Knifs, and Orbit now plays with a band called Saturn V, which contributed a *Ventures in Space*–like instrumental "Voyage Around the Moon" to the 1996 movie about 1960s music, *That Thing You Do*.

Also carrying on the "Ghoulardi connection" with popular music was drummer Michael Weldon, who played in the Mirrors, Styrenes, and Ex-Blank-Ex before turning his attention to pop culture in its many forms through his writings on psychotronics. Weldon's magazine *Psychotronic* has included several articles on Ghoulardi, among them a posthumous tribute, and Weldon has insisted to a national audience that "the best horror host was in Cleveland."

Those words mean more and more as Weldon's reputation as an expert on fringe movies and weird pop icons continues to grow through his magazine and books such as *The Psychotronic Encyclopedia of Film* and *The Psychotronic Video Guide*. In a 1996 interview with *Scene* magazine, Weldon cited as his biggest influences Forrest Ackerman's *Famous Monsters of Filmland* magazine (central to the revival of interest in horror movies among 1950s and 1960s young people), and Ghoulardi.

"I loved everything about that show," said Weldon. "I never missed it.... I loved him and his character, the music, and the movies that he played. If they repeated the same movie four times, I watched it four times." In a 1997 Ghoulardi tribute issue, Weldon wrote, "More than anybody, he was the inspiration for *Psychotronic.*"

Meanwhile, down in Canton, Dave Little stood in front of his ancient two-inch videotape machines, not far from a film projector, transferring ancient Ghoulardi recordings to modern formats, and loving every minute of it.

Little is one of the most important Ghoulardi fans because he is helping to preserve the surviving video pieces of the Ghoulardi legend so potential fans can see them in the future. His day job is owning a remote-broadcast truck and working in conjunction with the production company Image Video, but his joys include the huge, old-fashioned videotape machines he rescued from the trash heaps of local TV stations. The old TV programs, if they were recorded at all, were recorded on film or now-obsolete two-inch-wide videotape format. Little offers one of the few resources for transferring the old, and occasionally deteriorating, tapes to the newer formats.

He has transferred hours of tape for Schodowski, including portions of Ernie's work, and helped restore some skits that were showing signs of age. Though he does not attribute his fascination with broadcasting to Ghoulardi—that began when he saw a radio announcer doing a remote broadcast from a Humble Oil gas station when he was nine years old—Little still asserts that "Ghoulardi had a tremendous impact on a whole generation of us."

In his business, Little has done work for both the Clinton and Bush campaigns. Still, he said, "If I had an opportunity to dub tapes for Ghoulardi that I had never seen before, or to do something for either of the presidents, it's a no-brainer. I'm doing Ghoulardi stuff."

I DRANK
a MANNERS
BiG GHOULARDi ©

© COPYRIGHT STORER BROADCASTING CO. 1963

One afternoon in June, Cristina Ferrare was talking about what people liked about her hosting work on the Family Channel's *Home and Family* series. "I'm honest," said Ferrare, who grew up in Parma Heights, "and I say what I feel. I hide nothing. I'm not afraid to stand up for what I believe in. I'll say things that normal people will not say on television." A moment later the conversation turned to Ernie. "I loved Ghoulardi," Ferrare said. "I used to watch him all the time. . . . From the time I was a child, every Friday night I would sit by myself and watch Ghoulardi and get scared." Ferrare, who has been a model, actress, jet-setter, and TV personality, still said that when she met Ernie "to me, it was just, 'Wow, Ghoulardi, I can't believe it.'"

While Ferrare did not connect the dots between the anything-goes Ghoulardi and her own TV work, her producer, Woody Fraser, did. "Much like Ernie, she lets it all hang out," he said. And Ferrare's description of her on-air style more than slightly resembles Ernie's sense that Ghoulardi's honesty appealed to viewers.

More than thirty years after Ghoulardi hit Cleveland, audiences still seem to hunger for a bracing tonic of bluntness on TV. Some find that appetite satisfied by Howard Stern—although his preoccupations turn off as many as they attract. Others still wish for an antidote to the sycophancy that still marks hour after hour of TV.

In watching the more outspoken TV personalities of today—David Letterman, Rosie O'Donnell, Kathie Lee Gifford, Stern—people who grew up in 1960s Cleveland can recognize something they first tasted decades earlier.

As one fan said, Ghoulardi twisted a generation—and time has proven how clever his twist was. Not always funny, sometimes incoherent, often overlong or too "inside," Ghoulardi nonetheless was, and remains, something distinct and memorable.

Ernie's son Paul, an up-and-coming movie director, is stirring up trouble as eagerly as his father did. Paul's first movie, *Hard Eight,* came and went, but his second feature, *Boogie Nights,* was causing comment months before it was released. A look at the people working in and around the pornographic movie business in the '70s, the movie was the subject of eyebrow-raising stories about its subject, its male frontal nudity, and its two-and-a-half- to three-hour length. (Enough time, as *Entertainment Weekly* put it, for Debbie to do all of Dallas with time to spare.) Through the efforts of the twenty-six-year-old auteur, it also boasted a cast of solid players like Don Cheadle, Julianne Moore, and William H. Macy.

"The worst thing you can do is be wishy-washy," Paul said of moviemaking. His old man seems to have lived his whole life by that code, and Paul acknowledged "I definitely inherited that trait."

As *Boogie Nights* sat on the verge of national release, Paul said he was next considering making a film about his dad—one that would focus especially on his years as Ghoulardi. He already had paid tribute to his father by naming his production firm The Ghoulardi Film Company.

"It's a wonderful name," said Paul, who was born in Los Angeles after Ernie had retired the character to memory. "I was completely aware of it when I was a kid.... He could walk down the street here [in Los Angeles] and it didn't mean anything. But it became clear how big he was the second we stepped off the airplane [in Cleveland]—people stopping him there, people stopping him on the street.

"I said, 'Wow, he's not full of [bleep]. He was this huge thing.'"

Bibliography

BOOKS

Allen, Steve. *More Funny People*. New York: Stein & Day, 1982.

Barabas, SuzAnne, and Gabor Barabas. *Gunsmoke: A Complete History*. Jefferson, N.C.: McFarland & Co., 1990.

Bergreen, Laurence. *Look Now, Pay Later: The Rise of Network Broadcasting*. New York: Mentor/New American Library, 1981.

Bonchek, Herman, ed. *Cleveland: Annual Report 1963-64*.

Brooks, Tim, and Earle Marsh. *The Complete Directory to Prime Time Network and Cable TV Shows 1946-Present*. 6th ed. New York: Ballantine Books, 1995.

Case, Brian, and Stan Britt. *The Illustrated Encyclopedia of Jazz*. New York: Salamander/Harmony, 1978.

Condon, George. *Cleveland: The Best Kept Secret*. Cleveland: J.T. Zubal & P.D. Dole, Publishers, 1981.

Douglas, Mike. *Mike Douglas: My Story*. New York: Putnam's, 1978.

Fuldheim, Dorothy. *A Thousand Friends*. Garden City, N.Y.: Doubleday, 1974.

Jancik, Wayne, and Tad Lathrop. *Cult Rockers*. New York: Fireside, 1995.

Goldberg, Lee. *Unsold Television Pilots 1955-1988*. Jefferson, N.C.: McFarland & Co., 1990.

Maltin, Leonard. *Leonard Maltin's 1996 Movie & Video Guide*. New York: Signet, 1995.

Nash, Jay Robert, and Stanley Ralph Ross. *The Motion Picture Guide*. Chicago: Cinebooks, 1988.

Nite, Norm M. *Rock On: The Illustrated Encyclopedia of Rock 'N' Roll, The Solid Gold Years*. New York: Harper & Row, 1982.

——————, with Ralph M. Newman. *Rock On: The Illustrated Encyclopedia of Rock 'N ' Roll, The Modern Years, 1964-Present*. New York: Thomas Y. Crowell, 1978.

Robbins, Ira A., ed. *The Trouser Press Guide to '90s Rock*. 5th ed. New York: Fireside, 1997.

Van Tassel, David D., and John J. Grabowski, eds. *The Encyclopedia of Cleveland History*. 2nd ed. Bloomington, Ind.: Indiana University Press, 1996.

Watson, Elena M. *Television Horror Movie Hosts*. Jefferson, N.C.: McFarland & Co., 1991.

Weldon, Michael J. *The Psychotronic Video Guide*. New York: St. Martin's/Griffin, 1996.

Whitburn, Joel. *The Billboard Book of Top 40 Hits*. 6th ed. New York: Billboard Publications, 1996.

MAGAZINES, NEWSPAPERS, AND OTHER PERIODICALS

The following list includes the major periodical sources used in this book. Portions of other columns, newspaper stories, advertisements, letters, and TV listings in Cleveland's *News, Press,* and *Plain Dealer* and Akron's *Beacon Journal* also provided research information, as did 1963–64 listings in *TV Guide*.

ANONYMOUS ARTICLES

"Bob Wells Leaves for TV Job in Fla." *Cleveland Press*, May 24, 1979.

"Divorce Suit Bars Ghoulardi from His Home." *Cleveland Press*, February 12, 1964.

"Fireworks and Polish Jokes." *Scene*, October 25, 1973.

"Forecaster Goddard to Return Here." *The Plain Dealer*, September 4, 1965.

"Frank Sinatra Sends Roses to Donna." *The Plain Dealer*, February 1, 1965.

"Ghoulardi Goes West with Thrill Movies for Knifs." *Cleveland Press*, September 27, 1963.

"Ghoulardi Inc. Ends with Judge's Ruling." *Cleveland Press*, October 21, 1963.

"Ghoulardi Inc. Ordered by Court to Stop Selling." *Cleveland Press*, Sept. 20, 1963.

"Ghoulardi 'Stars' Play Final Game." *Euclid Journal*, Sept. 8, 1964.

"Hey Group! It's Ghoulardi!" *Monsterscene*, No. 2, not dated.

"Hoolihan is Heading to Dixie." *The Plain Dealer*, May 24, 1979.

"Hoolihan's Other Partner." *The Plain Dealer*, May 28, 1978.

"It's All a Gag." *Cleveland Press*, April 24, 1969.

"Mayor Apologizes to Fans for Ghoulardi's Absence." *Cleveland Press*, August 2, 1966.

"Remember Flash Gordon? He's Still Rushing to the Rescue." *Parma Post*, March 10, 1966.

"There's No Place Like Parma." *Parma Post*, March 31, 1966.

"Weird Excuse Wins Sympathy of Judge." *Cleveland Press*, August 22, 1963.

"What Catches the Teen-age Mind." *Time*, September 27, 1963.

"WJW Strike under Mediation." *The Plain Dealer*, November 17, 1963.

"Wooing the Voters." *The Plain Dealer*, May 28, 1980.

"You'd Find Life a Scream If You Opened Ghoulardi's Mail." *The Plain Dealer*, July 20, 1963.

BYLINED ARTICLES

Ascher-Walsh, Rebecca. "The Naked and the Dread." *Entertainment Weekly*, April 25, 1997.

Barrett, Bill. "Beverly Hillbillies Romp on Top of Ridge in the Nielsen Ratings." *Cleveland Press*, November 18, 1963.

——————. "Comedy Team to Reunite for a Special This Fall." *Cleveland Press*, June 2, 1965.

——————. "Ghoulardi's All-Stars at Bat for Charity." *Cleveland Press*, April 29, 1966.

——————. "'Ghoulardi' Will Be Emmy Host." *Cleveland Press*, May 12, 1981.

——————. "Man From UNCLE Pops By in Ghastly Ghoulardi Film." *Cleveland Press*, March 3, 1965.

——————. "Martin and Howard Pledge Lives, Fortunes to Parma." *Cleveland Press*, March 10, 1966.

——————. "More Cheap Movies for More Cities is Horror in Prospect." *Cleveland Press*, Sept. 13,1963.

——————. "Parma People Not Pleased Parma Place Perished." *Cleveland Press*, March 14,1966.

——————. "Parma's Patrons Place Parma Place in Purgatory." *Cleveland Press*, March 8, 1966.

Beam, Alvin. "Ghoulardi Still Going Strong." *The Plain Dealer*, March 29, 1964.

——————. "'Ghoulardi' Thrives on Hollywood 'Bombs'." *The Plain Dealer*, August 11, 1963.

——————. "What's to Do About Ghoulardi?" *The Plain Dealer*, June 30, 1963.

Bifoss, Fawn. "Ghoulish Success Mixes Kitsch With Kiszka." *Detroit Free Press*, March 20, 1977.

Calta, Louis. "Pete Myers, 40, of WNEW Is Dead." *New York Times*, Oct. 5, 1968.

Clark, Don. *Ghoul Pardi*, No. 1-20, Spring 1991 to Winter 1995/Spring 1996. Newsletter "for TV ghost host fans" by Ghoulardi fan from Barberton, Ohio.

Crooker, Mike, "Staying Sick: Michael Weldon's Psychotronic Cleveland Experience," *Scene*, October 24, 1996.

DeLuca, David, "The Mad, Mad Daddy." *Cleveland Magazine*, September 1984.

Dyer, Bob. "The Voice That Struck Gold." *Beacon Magazine (Akron Beacon Journal)*, April 25, 1993.

Eyman, Scott. "The After Hours Show." *The Plain Dealer Magazine*, not dated, ca. 1975.

——————. "Reflections of a Cool Ghoul." *Ohio Magazine*, 1975.

Feran, Tom. "Ghoulardi's Back for Appearance on Joe Bob's Drive-In." *The Plain Dealer*, October 12, 1991.

——————. "Recalling Laughs with 'Ghoulardi.'" *The Plain Dealer*, February 13, 1997.

——————. "Memorials Planned for Anderson." *The Plain Dealer*, February 8, 1997.

——————. "Through the Decades with Cleveland Television." *Plain Dealer magazine*, October 6, 1991.

——————. "TV Icon 'Ghoulardi' Dies at 73." *The Plain Dealer*, February 7, 1997.

GHOULARDi Bibliography

Fischer, Ruth, "No Place for Satire." *The Nation,* April 18, 1966.

Flanagan, James B. "Ernie's Special Worth a Look." *The Plain Dealer,* October 21, 1965.

———. "Funny Man Conway Cheers Grouch Club." *The Plain Dealer,* 1966.

Ford, Stephen. "Today . . . The Ghoul." *Detroit News,* July 31, 1977.

Frankel, Jim. "Will the Real Ernie Anderson Please Stand Up?" *Cleveland Press,* April 28, 1963.

Gitlin, Bob. "Ghoulardi Then and Now." *The Plain Dealer* magazine, November 18, 1990.

Hart, Raymond P. "Ghoulardi Returns for Evening of Fun." *The Plain Dealer,* August 13, 1970.

Heldenfels, R. D. "A Most Ghoulish Guru." *Akron Beacon Journal,* February 7, 1997.

———. "Area Fans to Salute Late Ghoulardi With Convention." *Akron Beacon Journal,* March 14, 1997.

Hickey, Bill. "Ghoulardi Strikes Gold in Hollywood." *The Plain Dealer,* March 5, 1978.

Lake, Richard. "Not Working Paid off Big." *Akron Beacon Journal,* January 14, 1962.

Major, Jack. "Ghoulardi's a Surprise Smash." *Akron Beacon Journal,* April 7, 1963.

———. "Mike Douglas: He's Sitting Atop the Heap." *Akron Beacon Journal,* May 16,1965.

Markey, Sanford. "Hottest Ghoul in Town." *Variety,* May 22, 1963.

Mayes, Gina. "He Keeps Ghouling and Ghouling." *Akron Beacon Journal,* October 31, 1993.

Mellow, Jan. "'Mad Daddy' Bails Out into Bale of Publicity." *The Plain Dealer,* June 15, 1958.

Minch, John J. "Weather Shows Are 'Overcast'." *The Plain Dealer,* July 18, 1965.

———. "Ghoulardi's Charade Has Become Bigger Than Life." *The Plain Dealer,* August 26, 1965.

Mudrak, Barbara. "Paaarma! Ghoulardi's Loony Legacy Lives." *Akron Beacon Journal,* October 13, 1980.

Olszewski, Mike. "Ghoulardi Rules Cleveland!" *Outre,* No. 8, not dated.

Peters, Harriet. "Ghoulardi Cools It in Hollywood Jaunt." *Cleveland Press,* August 7, 1964.

———. "Hey Group, Ghoulardi Rides Again." *Cleveland Press,* April 30, 1971.

———. "The Monster Who Dared." *Cleveland Press,* May 28, 1965.

———. "Two Ghouls Replace Ghoulardi in Strike." *Cleveland Press,* November 19, 1963.

Reesing, Bert J., "Ghoulardi No Longer Big Wheel." *The Plain Dealer,* November 3, 1963.

———. "'Ghoulardi' Quitting." *The Plain Dealer,* November 15, 1966.

———. "Time Running Out on Ghoulardi." *The Plain Dealer,* October 14, 1963.

Snauffer, Douglas. "The Bizarre Always Intrigued Son of Ghoul." *Akron Beacon Journal,* June 11, 1989.

Sweed, Ron. "Turn Blue Forever! The Ghoul Remembers Ghoulardi." *Scene,* February 13–19, 1997.

Walders, Joe. "Is There Life After Ghoulardi?" *Cleveland Magazine,* December 1975.

Weldon, Michael J. "Stay Sick With Ghoulardi." *Psychotronic,* not dated.

———, ed. *Psychotronic.* Issue No. 25, 1997, includes an extended posthumous tribute, "Ghoulardi Sez: Stay Sick and Turn Blue—Fink!" with discussion of Ghoulardi, the movies, the music, and post-Ghoulardi hosts.

Widman, Richard C. "It's Friday. Time for those Crazy Zany Boys on Channel 8." *The Plain Dealer,* August 22, 1986.

Wootten, Dick. "Ghoulardi Mixes with Film Hippies." *Cleveland Press,* July 3, 1967.

Wyler, Linda. "Canton TV 'Ghoul' Is Vindicated." *Akron Beacon Journal,* April 29, 1989.

RADIO BROADCASTS

Ernie Anderson. Interview by Morrie Zryl, WWWE (1100 AM), October 31, 1987.

Ernie Anderson. Radio interview with Tom Snyder, 1989.

Chris Quinn with Chuck Schodowski, Ron Sweed, Mike Olszewski. Ernie Anderson tribute. WMJI (105.7 FM), 1997.

RECORDS, CDS, AND TAPES

Conway, Tim, and Ernie Anderson. *are we on?* Liberty, 1967.

———. with Ernie Anderson. *Bull!* Liberty, 1967.

Cramps. *Songs the Lord Taught Us,* IRS, 1980.

———. *Stay Sick!* Enigma, 1990.

Easter Monkeys. *The Splendor of Sorrow.* Hit & Run, 1992

VIDEOTAPES, COMMERCIALLY DISTRIBUTED

The Best of Big Chuck and Lil' John, The Legend Continues: Volume 1. Gillett Communications of Ohio, 1993

The Best of Big Chuck and Lil' John, The Legend Continues:Volume 2. New World Communications of Ohio, 1994.

Time Warp: 1954. MPI Home Video.

Tunnelvision. 1976. Movie with performances by Ernie and Edwina Anderson. From Hollywood's Attic home video.

VIDEOTAPES, BROADCAST, AND PERSONAL COLLECTIONS

Tapes collected by Chuck Schodowski of Ernie Anderson and Ghoulardi performances include the known eighteen minutes of Ernie Anderson talking to viewers as Ghoulardi and the following additional material:

"Dizzy Discs"—Tim Conway lip-synching; Laubs soft twist bread commercial with Ernie Anderson and Conway; suspense thriller movie package opening; *Ernie's Place,* "Bullfighter" skit with Ernie Anderson and Tim Conway; *Ernie's Place,* Ernie Anderson interviews Andy Griffith; Anderson and Conway recording *are we on?* at Bowling Green State University— "Indians," "Superman," "Race Car Driver"; movie festival for women promotional spot with Anderson; Conway on *The Danny Kaye Show; Ernie Anderson Show* (special) selections; Millbrook bread commercials.

Also, Ernie Anderson interviews Ghoulardi; "Indians pitching coach" skit with Ernie Anderson and Chuck Schodowski; "Parma Place" installments: "The Piano" (episode 1), "Package," "Cheez Whiz," "Muck Raking"; Star Muffler commercial with Anderson, Schodowski; Ghoulardi filmed skits: "The Stranger," "The Date," "Stronger Than Dirt," "The Grocer," "Haunted House," "Bowling."

Ernie Anderson and Tim Conway visit *Hoolihan & Big Chuck;* Anderson and Conway perform "Race Car Driver" bit on *Hoolihan & Big Chuck;* film of the Ghoulardi All-Stars in action.

Big Chuck and Lil' John (WJW Channel 8) presented a tribute to Ernie Anderson in February 1997.

From Ron Sweed's film collection came self-shot movies of behind-the-scenes activity before and during Ghoulardi telecasts.

From Mike Olszewski of WOIO (Channel 19)/WUAB (Channel 43) came the raw footage of his interview with Ernie Anderson in 1996.

WEWS (Channel 5) broadcast "Remembering Dorothy," a series of features on commentator Dorothy Fuldheim in May 1997.

WEB SITES

The Cleveland Live! Web site, www.cleveland.com, and especially its section on Cleveland music of the past (www.cleveland.com/ultrafolder/music/timeline). The official Cramps Web site is www.loop.com/~hellione/cramps.html. A brief description of the "Purple Knif Show" CD is at www.media.mit.edu/push/knif.html. The band Saturn V can be read about at www.sirius.com.

GHOULARDi
Bibliography

Photo Credits

Frequently cited sources are referred to by the following codes; all other sources are cited below with full name.

Auth–Authors' collection
CSU–Cleveland Press Collection, Cleveland State University Archives
Macoska–Photo by Janet Macoska
Schodowski–Chuck Schodowski collection
Sweed–Ron Sweed collection
Press–The Cleveland Press
HA–Hollywood's Attic

FRONT MATTER   p. 2–CSU; p. 5–Schodowski; p. 6 (top left)–Schodowski; p. 6 (upper left)–Sweed; p. 6 (lower left)–Schodowski; p. 6 (bottom left)–Schodowski; p. 6 (top center)–Schodowski; p. 6 (center)–Sweed; p. 6 (bottom center)–Auth; p. 6 (top right)–Schodowski; p. 6 (middle right)–Schodowski; p. 6 (bottom right)–Sweed; p. 9–Sweed.

CHAPTER 1   p. 12–Schodowski; p. 14 (left)–Schodowski; p. 14 (right)–Schodowski; p. 15 (top)–Sweed; p. 15 (bottom)–Sweed; p. 16 (top)–Sweed; p. 16 (center)–Sweed; p. 16 (bottom)–Schodowski; p. 17 (top)–CSU; p. 17–Schodowski; p. 18 (left)–Sweed; p. 18 (right)–Schodowski; p. 19 (top)–Schodowski; p. 19 (bottom)–Sweed.

CHAPTER 2   p. 20–Schodowski; p. 22–Schodowski; p. 23–Schodowski; p. 24–CSU; p. 25–Sweed; p. 26 (top left)–Schodowski; p. 26 (bottom left)–Schodowski; p. 26 (right)–CSU; p. 27–Schodowski; p. 28–Schodowski; p. 29–CSU; p. 32–Schodowski; p. 33–CSU; p. 35–CSU.

CHAPTER 3   p. 38–Schodowski; p. 40–Schodowski; p. 41–Auth; p. 43 (top)–Schodowski; p. 43 (bottom)–Auth; p. 44–CSU; p. 41–Schodowski; p. 46–Sweed; p. 47–Auth; p. 48 (top)–Auth; p. 48 (center)–Auth; p. 48 (bottom)–Auth; p. 49–Schodowski; p. 50–Auth; p. 52–53–CSU; p. 53–Auth; p. 55–Auth; p. 56–CSU; p. 56–CSU; p. 57–CSU; p. 59 (top)–Schodowski; p. 59 (bottom)–Schodowski; p. 61–The Plain Dealer p. 62–Sweed; p. 63–Sweed; p. 64–Auth; p. 65–Schodowski; p. 66–Schodowski.

CHAPTER 4   p. 68–CSU; p. 70–Sweed; p. 72–CSU; p. 74 (top)–CSU; p. 74 (center)–CSU; p. 74 (bottom)–CSU; p. 75 (top right)–CSU; p. 75 (center right)–CSU; p. 75 (bottom)–CSU; p. 76 (top)–CSU; p. 76 (bottom)–CSU; p. 77–CSU; p. 78–Sweed.

CHAPTER 5   p. 80–Sweed; p. 82–Ralph Gulko collection; p. 83–Sweed; p. 84–Schodowski; p. 85–CSU; p. 86 (top)–Macoska; p. 86 (center)–Macoska; p. 86 (bottom right)–Macoska; p. 87 (top)–Sweed; p. 87 (center)–Sweed; p. 87 (bottom)–Macoska; p. 89–Schodowski; p. 90–Press; p. 91–Sweed; p. 92–Sweed; p. 93 (top)–Sweed; p. 93 (bottom)–Sweed; p. 94 (top)–Schodowski; p. 94 (bottom)–CSU; p. 95–Macoska; p. 97 (top left)–CSU; p. 97 (bottom left)–CSU; p. 97 (top right)–CSU; p. 98–Sweed; p. 99 (top)–Schodowski; p. 99 (bottom)–CSU; p. 100 (top left)–Schodowski; p. 100 (center left)–Schodowski; p. 100 (bottom right)–Macoska; p. 101 (top)–Schodowski; p. 101 (bottom)–Sweed; p. 102 (top)–Schodowski; p. 102 (bottom)–Schodowski; p. 103–Schodowski; p. 105–Sweed.

CHAPTER 6   p. 106–Schodowski; p. 108–Schodowski; p. 110 (left)–Schodowski; p. 110 (right)–Schodowski; p. 111–Schodowski; p. 112 (top left)–Schodowski; p. 112 (center left)–Schodowski; p. 112 (bottom left)–Schodowski; p. 112 (top center)–Schodowski; p. 112 (center)–Schodowski; p. 112 (bottom center)–Schodowski; p. 112 (top right)–Schodowski; p. 112 (center right)–Schodowski; p. 112 (bottom right)–Schodowski; p. 113–Schodowski; p. 114–Schodowski; p. 115–Sweed; p. 116–Schodowski; p. 118 (left)–Press; p. 118 (right)–Press; p. 120–Schodowski.

CHAPTER 7   p. 122–Sweed; p. 124–Schodowski; p. 125–Sweed; p. 126–CSU; p. 127–Schodowski; p. 129–Schodowski; p. 131–Schodowski

CHAPTER 8   p. 132–CSU; p. 134–Schodowski; p. 135 (top)–Schodowski; p. 135 (center)–CSU; p. 135 (bottom)–Sweed; p. 136–Schodowski; p. 138–Sweed; p. 142–Sweed; p. 143–Sweed; p. 146–Schodowski; p. 147–Schodowski; p. 148–HA; p. 148–HA; p. 151–Sweed; p. 151–The Plain Dealer.

EPILOGUE   p. 152–Schodowski; p. 155 (top left)–Macoska; p. 155 (bottom left)–Macoska; p. 155 (top right)–Macoska; p. 155 (bottom right)–Macoska; p. 158–Schodowski; p. 159 (top right)–Press; p. 159 (bottom)–Sweed; p. 160 (top left)–Auth; p. 160 (upper left)–Auth; p. 160 (lower left)–Macoska; p. 160 (bottom left)–Sweed; p. 160(top center)–CSU; p. 160 (center)–Macoska; p. 160 (bottom center)–Schodowski; p. 160 (top right)–Schodowski; p. 160 (center right)–Schodowski; p. 160 (bottom right)–Sweed.

GHOULARDI
Photo Credits

Index

THIS KNIF DRANK a MANNERS BiG GHOULARDi ©

GHOULARDi

Index

GHOULARDI

Index

ABOUT THE AUTHORS

Tom Feran is television critic of *The Plain Dealer* and former president of the Television Critics Association. A reporter and editor for 20 years, he is a graduate of St. Ignatius High School in Cleveland and Harvard College, where he was president and editor of *The Lampoon*. He and his wife have four children.

R.D. Heldenfels has been a professional writer for 25 years. His work has appeared in newspapers in Virginia and New York as well as in *Cablevision*, *TV Guide*, *Total Television* and other magazines. He has written mainly about television for more than 15 years, is a former president of the Television Critics Association and has been the television writer for the *Akron Beacon Journal* since 1994. A graduate of Princeton University, he is the author of one previous book, *Television's Greatest Year: 1954* (Continuum, 1994). He lives in Mogadore, Ohio, with his sons Brendan and Conor.

Designed by Laurence J. Nozik

"STAY SICK"
GOULARDI